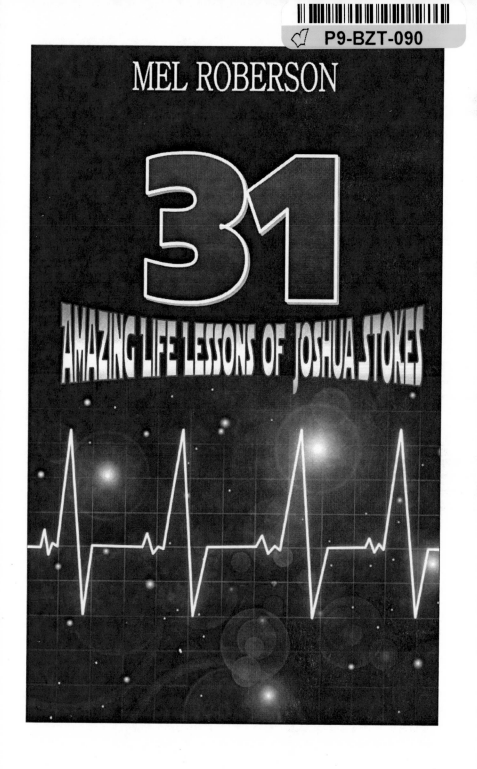

MEL ROBERSON

31

AMAZING LIFE LESSONS OF JOSHUA STOKES

31

AMAZING LIFE LESSONS OF
JOSHUA STOKES

MEL ROBERSON

31 AMAZING LIFE LESSONS OF JOSHUA STOKES

Cover design by: GreeneHouse Media, Print Division
Website: www.GreeneHouseMedia.com

ISBN: 978-0-9828180-3-9

FIG Publishing
12138 Central Avenue, #464
Mitchellville, Maryland 20721
1.888.202.6766
www.FIGPublishing.com
info@FIGPublishing.com

FIG Publishing
Maryland

DEDICATION

This book is dedicated to everyone who has touched my life in a positive way. More specifically, I must give special thanks to God, my parents (Mel, Sr. & Dee), my brother (Dave), and my kids (Ally & Rae) who have always loved me unconditionally.

Also, I must say thank you to Ann Bergman, the professor in college that gave me my first personal development audio cassettes. I still have them!

Ridgley Pearson, one of my college English professors, saw my potential and pushed me to write even when I didn't want to. Rest in peace. I miss you dearly.

Wilburn Smith, a business mentor who taught me that my past does not equal my future. Rest peacefully, Uncle Wilburn. Wish you were here to continue sharing your insights and to see who I've grown into so far.

To my supporters, may God bless you, and thank YOU for reading my labor of love.

FOREWORD

31 Amazing Life Lessons of Joshua Stokes is a great easy read for folks of all ages. The lessons are reminders of things we probably already know, or have heard before, but need to hear again. Mel gives it to you straight... with a chaser. That's just how he is. Mel and I met while working on a film project a while ago. Confident, charming, caring, and intelligent, I knew that he had greatness within him by the way he carried himself. I grew an appreciation for his work ethic on and off the camera. Behind the scenes, he was always reading, eating healthy, and working out. Every day, he was looking for ways to become better at the things he was involved in. He lives the "31" daily. This isn't just a book, this is a lifestyle.

I'm very happy to know him as a friend, colleague, and now as an author! Have you ever had a person in your life who told you exactly what you needed to hear—and at the exact time you needed to hear it? Mel has a way of doing that, even when you don't want him to. He gives you the truth in an amazingly loving way. And with 31 he does it again. Valuable life lessons wrapped up in a riveting story. Mel pours out all the love and life and truth he can muster, and then some! He gives you the best that he's got from his whole heart and soul. He writes, he moves, he shares from a place of love and giving; gifting us with what he knows for sure. The book "31" is a wonderful read to be read again and again.

Karen Malina White
Actress/Activist/Avid Reader

A NOTE TO YOU, THE READER

Some years ago, a friend called to read a quote to me. This was an amazingly prolific quote that sounded like something from a famous motivational speaker or author. She asked me if I knew who said it. After guessing every name I could think of in the personal development industry, she revealed to me that I had said those words to her at a social event we both attended where she told me about her bad day. She went on to characterize my every day way of talking as 'these little Mel-isms that are always right on time.' She even commented that I should put them in a book.

With her encouragement, I started writing down all the little sayings I had used over the years. Even though I love books of quotes, I didn't think that was the format I wanted to use to share my thoughts. Next, I thought I would interview people who I thought lived the Mel-isms lessons/sayings that you will read in this book. That took a lot of time, and I still didn't know how to put a book together that would do these lessons justice. Finally, I was introduced to two books that changed my life, both as a person and as an author. *The Richest Man in Babylon* by George Clayson and *The Dream Giver* by Bruce Wilkerson. Both of these were personal development books written in story form. The images that the authors painted stuck with me for years. With this newfound inspiration, I decided to create an opportunity for the reader to hear 'Mel-isms' in a format they could remember and be drawn into – as a story. You are holding in your hands *31 Amazing Life Lessons of Joshua Stokes.*

By no stretch of the imagination is this book perfect, or even complete. All of our life lessons grow and morph as we mature as people, and because of this, I didn't want to die with my book still inside of me. A well-known speaker said, "You don't have to get it right, you just have to get it going." As time progresses, I'm sure that I will improve as a person and an author. My hope is that this book helps you to live a more fulfilling life as you decide and begin to LIVE THE 31.

Successfully yours,

Mel Roberson

BOOK 1

It was a day like any other Tuesday. Successful businessman Joshua Stokes got up early, went through his normal exercise routine, had a decent breakfast and protein shake, and prepared his briefcase for his business of the day. The morning news played in the background as he checked a few emails. The CD player in the bathroom always had some type of personal development audio in it. That was the only thing Josh would listen to while he shaved and showered. It mentally prepared him to face his day. It was his mantra... his way of living... it was part of his being. He was consistent and confident.

Stokes had built several different lucrative companies. A business magazine recently wrote an article about him, naming Joshua "Mr. Healthy, Wealthy, & Wise" for the year. The awards and accolades he had accumulated were amazing. The walls of his home office were filled with plaques and certificates. There were pictures of him with business people, political leaders, dignitaries, spiritual gurus, and just about any other important person you could name. Even though he knew people of high stature, Joshua Stokes was extremely down to earth. He was a humble man, and he had huge faith in God. He wasn't born with a silver spoon in his mouth. He worked for all that he had. Growing up in the inner city of Chicago gave him street smarts that added to his business savvy. Based on statistics, he shouldn't have made it this far. But Josh was a fighter. His parents always told him not to be an exception to the rule, just be exceptional. He was just that.

Before he left home, he would always call his two daughters, Tiffany and Miranda, on the phone to wish them a great day at school. They lived with their mom on the other side of town. He loved his kids with every fiber of his being. His marriage seemed to be the only thing that didn't work out for him. Outside of that, everything he touched turned to gold. He loved his daughters, he achieved a tremendous amount of success, he was in great shape, he had plans on getting married to a dance teacher at the local performing arts college; but he felt like something was missing. He didn't know what it was, and even worse he didn't know where to begin looking. He prayed every night for that uneasy feeling to leave him, but it never went away.

On this typical Tuesday, Josh took his typical route to make his typical deposit at Dow International Bank. Everything seemed to be in order. He stood in the line that would eventually lead him to Patti. She was his favorite teller at the bank, and his ad-hoc Spanish tutor. He always wanted to learn how to speak Spanish, and Patti agreed to teach him something new every time he came to the bank. She was an exchange student from Columbia who worked there to pay her way through school. She was also the person that told Joshua that he should meet her dance teacher, and for that he was truly grateful. She had no family here in America, and Mr. Stokes was one of the nicest people that she knew.

"Que onda amiga?" he said as he approached her window. (What's going on my friend?)

"Buenas dias senior! Como esta?" she replied. (Good morning sir. How are you?)

"Bien, bien... y tu?" Josh said with a smile. (Good, good... and you?)

"Asi asi." Patti said with a slight frown on her face. (So-so.)

Joshua had better people skills than most. His Spanish wasn't the best, but his ability to deal with people and make them feel important was incomparable to any other business man in the area. He was one of the good guys. Not only was he a leader in the business community, he was a friend to all who knew him. By the end of his banking transaction, Patti was smiling and ready to face her day with a new found enthusiasm. Even though Josh was going to see Vanessa Anderson later—his girlfriend and Patti's dance teacher—he gave Patti a little note in an envelope to give to Vanessa in class later on.

It was business as usual on this Tuesday morning. Joshua turned around from the counter and greeted a pregnant woman that was standing in line behind him. They exchanged smiles as he walked past her, but before he could get five feet away from her, six masked men walked into the bank, firing bullets into the air yelling, "This is a robbery! Nobody moves, nobody gets hurt! Get on the ground and don't look at us! Keep your hands where we can see them and your mouths shut! If you don't, that indicates to us that you want to lose your life!"

The entire place went hysterical. Joshua turned around and could see the fear in Patti's eyes. Even worse, the pregnant lady a few feet from him was crying and hyperventilating. The tears flowed down her cheeks like rivers. Her loud yells drew attention to her, and one of the masked men moved rapidly toward her and Joshua. He attempted to calm her down but it was to no avail. All the martial arts training Joshua had done was going to be tested at this very moment. Gun pointed in the pregnant woman's direction, the armed robber increased the speed of his steps with each shout that escaped her mouth. All that Josh could think about was his Jujitsu instructor telling him, "Luck favors the prepared." He played the next moment out in his head, giving himself a vivid picture of exactly what he wanted to happen. The gunman pulled back the hammer of his pistol when he was about a foot away from the pregnant woman. Joshua saw the opportunity to make a move, and he did. Just before the assailant pulled the trigger, Josh had him by the wrist. The only thing that he was thinking about was saving the life of the young pregnant woman. Patti was able to push the alarm button while Josh distracted the robbers. Two of the five remaining masked men guarded the door while the other three converged on the wrestling match between Josh and the criminal. None of the robbers had a clear shot at Josh because he and the robber were rolling around frantically on the floor. All of a sudden… "BLAOW BLAOW" - two gun shots rang out. The gunman that Josh was wrestling with jumped up and all six robbers dashed out of the bank as Joshua Stokes lay there silently staring at the ceiling. His vision began to blur and eventually he fell unconscious.

The police and several ambulances arrived at the scene within minutes. The team of robbers had managed to escape. Patti was in tears. Every single person that was in the bank was shaken up. The pregnant lady almost went into labor. Josh had been shot. He was willing to give his life in an attempt to save another.

~~

I know what you're probably thinking… yes, I'm talking to you. More than likely you are saying to yourself, "What?! How can he die so soon? I was just getting to know Josh! I liked him! No, this isn't right! I don't even want to read any more!" Well my friend, it's not over yet. In many cases what looks like the end is only the beginning. Josh did get shot. He has a bullet lodged in his brain. But he's not dead; at least, not yet. Do you want to learn more? Do you really want to know what his life will be like in the state that he's in? You've come this far, why give up now? The spirit of Joshua Stokes can only live on if you continue reading.

THE VISITATION

The mid-day news was filled with the story of Joshua Stokes, the successful business man who had given his life to save the lives of others. But he wasn't dead. Josh had fallen into a coma. His family and his closest friends had been informed about the incident before he even left the bank, and anybody that didn't know found out when the news cast aired. He was well respected and borderline famous. His brother Donavan Stokes and good friend Gregory H. Branson III were two of the first people at the hospital. His girlfriend Vanessa arrived shortly after the men, and Tiffany and Miranda were pulled out of school to come see their dad. Because Joshua was so well known, the waiting room of the hospital was filled with people that loved him. The best doctors in the area had been assembled to assess the situation and try to save his life. The way that the bullet was lodged in his brain made it difficult for them to reach it. One of the specialists even suggested it would be better to leave the bullet where it was lodged and just pray for the best.

Josh was not the type to give up easily, but it seemed as if fate had dealt him a poor hand in the card game of life. Was this frightful Tuesday the reason that he had been having that uneasy feeling? Was his intuition trying to warn him somehow? Who really knows? The important thing was that he was still alive. His cheerleading squad sat patiently in the waiting room with baited breath, anxious to hear the doctors' decision about their beloved Joshua Stokes. Less than an hour after he arrived, the decision was made to go ahead and operate.

Josh was on the operating room table with his body connected to all types of machines and tubes. He could hear, but could not see or talk. It was as if his conscious mind was surrounded by a black abyss where he could listen to the outside world, but could not communicate with it. He felt like he was floating in outer space. You would think that a person with a bullet encamped in his skull would be experiencing a tremendous amount of suffering, but the only real pain that Josh felt was the pain of not being able to speak to his daughters and the other people that he loved. He heard one of the doctors in the room talking about him, saying to another, "One little slip-up and this man will be a vegetable with no use of his body at all. He may even become brain-dead. The odds are a million to one that we will be able to pull through, because the longer we wait, the worse he will get."

Those statistics didn't sound like good odds to Joshua. He debated with himself whether he wanted to live or not. The man performing the operation didn't have a good attitude about the procedure, and Josh couldn't give a pep talk to the doctors before the team of surgeons cut him open. Pep talks were his specialty. The uneasy feeling that he had been experiencing for the past few months grew heavier by the second. He wasn't a quitter, but at that moment in time he had the feeling that this was his date with destiny. A nurse hurried into the room and told the other specialists that Dr. Fatima Elkordy agreed to come in and perform the surgery. She was a neurosurgeon from Egypt, and had met Stokes at an "Ending World Hunger" event a few years earlier. It would take her about a day to get to Chicago from Egypt though. Josh knew that if anybody could pull it off, it was her. The only problem was that every moment that went decreased his chances of living. He was at peace and happy on the inside, but showed no signs of improvement on the outside. That's when it happened: The brightest light that Josh had ever seen filled the room. That's when Josh got his vision and speech back. He could see, he could talk, he could move. He jumped up off the table and began to speak to the doctors proclaiming that a miracle had happened, but they couldn't hear him, they couldn't even see him. Well, at least not the "him" that was chasing them around the operating room. Then Josh looked at the table and saw that his body was still there. This scared him, and he began to scream at the top of his lungs. A voice spoke to him from behind him in the far corner of the room saying, "They can't hear you Mr. Stokes."

Startled, Josh turned around and immediately went into a martial arts fighting stance. He was confused and angry at the same time. His anger and confusion did not compare to his disbelief though. He was astonished to see an angel with beautiful extended wings sitting on a chair in the corner of the room. The figure's clothing was brighter than anything he had ever seen before. It was like a scene out of a sci-fi movie. The angel stood up and offered his hand to Joshua, trying to greet him with a handshake. Josh didn't know what to do. Should he run, should he fight, or should he ask questions? Ninety-four percent of people in that situation would run and scream, but Josh knew that nobody could hear him so that served no purpose. Five percent of people would fight, but Josh had done enough fighting for the day. It's what got him in this situation in the first place. That left 1 percent who would ask questions, and that's exactly what he did.

"Who are you?" Josh asked in a commanding voice.

"I'm an angel," said the gentleman in the corner.

"Thanks Captain Obvious!" exclaimed Josh.

"My name is Logan, if that's what you're asking, and I'm an Angel."

"Logan? Like the comic book character Wolverine Logan?"

"I'm an Angel. I've been around longer than the X-Men, but yes my name is Logan."

This was no longer the typical Tuesday for Joshua Stokes. Out of all the people he had ever met, none of them were angels. At least not in the form that Logan was. "So are you going to shake my hand?" Logan asked with a slight smile. This was no laughing matter to Josh though. Stokes glanced at his body on the operating table, then at Logan, then back at his body again. "Am I dead, Mr. Logan?" he asked as he fell to the floor and sat with his head in his hands. "Dr. Elkordy is on her way and I died before she got here. I lived a good life. I wish I could have said goodbye to my daughters. They are my only real reason for living. I've provided for them though. They will have plenty of money to survive…"

"Josh, please stop rambling." Logan interrupted. "You're not dead yet, but if you feel you have nothing else to live for you can die now. I can have it arranged if you want to just give up… or there is an alternative. I was sent here to take you on a bit of a journey - that is, if you want to go. You're in a coma, Josh. It will take you about a month or so to recover. I will take you to several moments in your life that made a significant impact on you. At the end of our voyage, you will have to make a decision. The longer you wait, the longer it takes. Would you like to get started?"

"Wait, wait, wait! You can't just expect me to be OK with this! I'm in the hospital looking at my body on an operating table. I'm having a conversation with what appears to be an angel. This wasn't exactly on my list of things to do today, Mr. Logan." Josh shouted.

"Please, just call me Logan. 'Mr.' sounds so formal. If I was the comic book character, would you call me 'Mr. Logan' or 'Mr. Wolverine'? Logan is fine," said the Angel.

The conversation between Josh and Logan didn't go on much longer. Josh was always a man of action, and even though he was somewhat afraid, the trip with Logan seemed more interesting than just sitting in the operating room looking at his body on the table. He had nothing to lose except his life, and he may lose that anyway. Hours had passed since the incident at the bank. Dr. Elkordy was a day away from arriving, and there was no way for Josh to communicate with anyone else except for Logan. "So what do I have to do?" Josh asked.

Logan pulled out a small leather bound handbook, and began reading it to Josh. "Each day we will look at a different part of your life. Each event taught you something. It helped to make you into what you are today. After each event, write down what it was that you learned. What was the lesson, and if you want to, you can write down an example of the lesson outside of your own experience. As I told you before, you will have a decision to make at the end of all of your lessons. It's getting late, and an angel needs his beauty rest. I'll be back here first thing in the morning to start the journey." As soon as Logan finished speaking, he disappeared.

Josh looked around the operating room for Logan, but he was no longer there. He had forgotten that there were other people in there, attempting to save his life. He glanced at his body one more time, and then he left the operating room. As he walked through the halls of the hospital toward the waiting room, he began to feel extremely tired. He got to the waiting room and it was filled to capacity with news reporters, family, and friends. He was shocked to see so many people there awaiting the outcome of his future. Even though Josh had done so much to help other people, he never really thought anything of it. It was natural to him. His two daughters were there with their mother. He sat next to Tiffany and Miranda, wishing he could tell them not to cry and that everything was going to be all right, even though he wasn't sure of that himself. Josh sat there for the rest of the evening looking at his daughters until he fell asleep.

THE JOURNEY

DAY 1

"Good morning, Joshua!" Logan awakened Josh in a loud, booming voice.

"Not so loud! This isn't boot camp." Josh said.

"The early bird gets the worm, Mr. Stokes - or at least a piece of it," Logan laughed.

"I'm not partial to worms, and please call me Josh if I must call you Logan." Josh replied. "And where did my daughters go? Where am I?"

"This is the first day of our journey Josh. We are about to go to the bank. The day that you saved the pregnant woman's life." said Logan.

Instantly they were teleported into Dow International Bank. It was the exact moment when Josh noticed the team of robbers. It didn't feel the same though. Josh was looking at the scene from a bird's eye view, so to speak. He could see himself passing the pregnant woman. He was outside of his body. He quickly turned to Logan and asked, "What's happening? Can I change what is about to happen? I'm here with you, and you're an angel. You have to have the power to do something, Logan!"

Logan replied, "We are simply here to watch and learn."

The event played out exactly how Josh remembered. The robbers came in, the pregnant woman started crying, one of the robbers approached her, Josh defended her and got shot. It was odd for him to see it from a different point of view. At the very moment when the gun went off that shot him in the head, Josh closed his eyes and yelled "STOP!" Everything in the bank was in suspended animation when Josh re-opened his eyes.

"What's happening, Logan?"

"You said stop... so everything stopped."

"This is too painful to watch, and there isn't anything for me to learn here."

"What were you feeling when all of this took place, Josh? You looked very brave to me."

"Brave? I was scared out of my mind!"

"But Josh, what you did was extremely courageous. You saved the woman's life. Not to mention her unborn child."

"I was afraid. I acted because I felt I had to. She was more afraid than I was. I would not have been able to stand there and watch her die."

Josh was overwhelmed. What could he possibly learn by watching the exact moment that may lead to his death? Logan just stood there expressionless. Josh turned to Logan and said, "I just don't get it." Logan completely understood what Josh was going through and replied, "Most people say the exact same thing when I take them through this. Mr. Stokes, what you have to understand is that you did a very noble thing. What you did was totally selfless. And the fact that you were afraid means nothing. Josh, courage is not the absence of fear. Courage is being afraid and acting anyway."

Tears welled up in Josh's eyes. He felt extremely tired. "Can we go now?" he asked. Logan agreed to leave and took Josh to what looked like some sort of college dorm room. It had a bed and a desk in it. Nothing fancy, just a place for him to write and to rest. On the desk, there was a stack of paper and several envelopes. He told Josh, "I know it was hard for you to see that, but it was the first place that we had to go. Get some rest, and we will start Day 2 once you are done resting. Oh, and by the way Josh, there was something that I forgot to mention when we first met. What you write down after each day will be delivered to somebody that you know or love. You won't know who, but it will be exactly what that person needs at that time in their life."

"So this is some sort of 'letters from the grave' exercise that you have me doing?" Josh asked, sounding slightly irritated.

"No Josh, but if what you learn can help other people, isn't it your duty to share it with them? The notes will be delivered via a special courier, and it will appear as if you wrote them long ago but just waited to have them delivered. By the way, you're not exactly dead yet. I'm leaving now. Enjoy the balance of your evening."

Josh sat at the desk and cried. He sat at the desk and began to think about what he just saw. As soon as he was able to clear his eyes, this is what he wrote:

Have Courage: Courage is not the absence of fear... Courage is being afraid and taking action anyway. When we are courageous, we grow! Take a step toward doing what you are afraid of doing. It will make you a better person. Run toward your challenges, because that is the only way to get through them! You never know who may be affected because you decided to act!

Josh took the note, folded it, put it in an envelope and left it on the desk, then went to sleep. While he slept, another angel came in the room and took the envelope.

DAY 2

Josh woke up before Logan arrived. He was used to exercising in the morning, but there was nothing in his small quarters for him to exercise with. He settled for some push-ups and sit-ups, but only after he had opened the door of the room he was in to see if there was anything around that looked interesting. There wasn't. When he opened the door to the room, he saw nothing but darkness and stars, as if he was in outer space. Logan finally arrived.

"Good morning, Josh," said Logan.

"Good morning Logan, if indeed it is morning," Josh replied.

"You must have opened the door. I hope you didn't freak out." Logan laughed.

"Let me see… I'm in a coma, but I can talk to angels that take me to different parts of my life, then bring me back to a jail cell in outer space! I think that freaking out is in order, sir!" Josh said in a very un-amused tone.

"Josh, I know it's not an easy concept for you to grasp. You would have to agree, though, that this is better than you being in the hospital not able to communicate with anybody at all. And the reason that your room seems to be in space is because of the way we have to travel through time."

"Whatever, Logan! Can we just get started please!?" replied the impatient Joshua Stokes.

"Sure," Logan said, and much more serious than he was before.

"I'm sorry to be so snappy Logan, but yesterday was really hard for me. I have a request."

"What would that be?" Logan asked.

"Can we go back to the bank today? I feel like I need to go back there again." This time Josh asked in a more humble tone.

Logan pulled out his rule book and said, "I wasn't going to tell you this until you had completed at least half of the events, but the rules say 'Each voyager has the opportunity to pick one day that they would like to go to.' So yes, we can go back to the bank. But do you really want to use that privilege this early?" said Logan.

"Yes, I do," Josh said.

In the blink of an eye, they were back at the bank. The events played out just as they did the first and second time Josh had seen them. Logan stood their quietly as Josh walked around the bank looking at different things. He was more aware this time and he took in every single detail that he could. He was particularly observant of his interactions with the masked gunman. This time, Josh watched everything up until the paramedics carried him to the ambulance, then he whispered, "Stop," and everything stopped just as it did the day before.

"Are you all right Josh?" asked Logan.

"Yes, I'm fine. I was afraid when all of this took place, but I wasn't worried," he replied.

"And why do you think that is?"

"Because of my faith."

"Go on," Logan said with a slight smile.

"I knew that there was a power greater than me at work. The fear was the human part of me, but my spiritual side wasn't worried about the outcome. I did what I was supposed to do," Josh said sounding relieved.

"Is there anything else that you would like to share?"

"No sir, just get me back to my intergalactic dorm room so I can write, please." Josh now had a smile on his face. "But why do I feel so tired after each event?"

"Time travel is hard for humans. Your concept of what a day is happens to be a little different here. So even though it only seems like we've been gone a short time, you've put in a full day's work," Logan explained.

They arrived in Josh's room just as miraculously as they had left. Logan said his goodbyes and left Josh alone to tend to his writings. After sitting on the bed for a few minutes, Josh went to the desk and began to write:

Remember that there is a power greater than you: We often forget that we were created by a Greater Power. Since we were created by that Power, we belong to that Power. Just like parents to children, God takes care of His o wn. Just remember that the challenges you face can be handled with the help of "your Parent" who is able to handle a lot more than we give Him credit for.

Josh took the note, folded it, put it in an envelope and left it on the desk, then went to sleep. While he slept, another angel came in the room and took the envelope.

DAY 3

Josh woke up early just as he did the day before and was a little excited to see what the lesson of the day was going to be. Logan arrived and found Josh 'bright-eyed and bushy-tailed.' He had already gone through his workout routine; well, at least the one that he could do in his small room. Today he was pleased to see Logan.

"Where are we off to today Logan?" Josh asked.

"Do you really want me to ruin the surprise?" replied Logan. "We'll be there in the blink of an..."

A split second later, Josh found himself at a basketball game in the gym of his old high school. "... eye!" Logan finished his statement.

It was the fourth quarter and there were three seconds left on the game clock. His high school team was down by two points. Josh's best friend, Greg, was one of the stars on the team. Josh was a good athlete, but he wasn't the star. He was decent in many different sports, but he knew his role in every game. The coach had the team in a tight circle so that he could map out the plan to win the game. The game-winning shot was to be taken by Greg. Josh was the one who would inbound the ball to him.

"Wow!" exclaimed Josh. "I remember this game like it was yesterday!" The two of them watched on as the five players from Josh's high school stepped onto the floor. As Josh and Logan sat in the stands, they could tell that there was a conversation going on between the younger Josh and Greg as they got ready for the final three seconds of the game.

"I don't want to take this shot, Josh. If I miss, we don't go to state semi-finals," Greg said.

"You have to Greg! You're the best player."

"It's not the same Josh. This game means something," Greg said, with a ton of anxiety in his voice.

"Look Greg, it's now or never. Just give it your best. For me, OK?" said Josh.

"OK, Josh. I can do it!" Greg said the words with more confidence in his voice.

They took the floor. Josh inbounded the ball just as the coach had set up the play. The final second ticked off the clock just as Greg released the ball. Everything seemed to be moving in slow motion. The gym was silent. The ball floated through the air with a nearly perfect backspin. It approached the rim and it looked like it was going to go in. It bounced off the front of the rim falling short by just a centimeter. In that moment, Josh's team lost the game, and it was over. The disappointed crowd began to exit the gym. The team went into the locker room so that the coaching staff could address them. Coach Womack, the head coach of the program, stood in the center of the circle to speak to the whole team.

"You guys played a great game. You gave it everything that you had, and I'm proud of you." Coach Womack went on to say. "I know that this…"

Greg interrupted, "I'm sorry Coach. I'm sorry team. I let you all down. I missed the shot, and I lost the game."

"Stop it, Branson! The loss didn't just go on your record, it went on our record. You did your best. In basketball, and in life, you have to shoot the shot!" Coach Womack explained.

Logan and the adult Joshua stood in the background listening. Joshua stood there in amazement of the knowledge that his coach was sharing with the team. He didn't realize how many life lessons he had learned from Coach Womack. Logan saw the gleam in Josh's eyes and tapped him on the shoulder. "We'll stay here until you decide it's time to leave," Logan said. Joshua wanted to stay there forever, but he knew that there were many more days ahead of him where he had to learn lessons. He agreed to leave and ended up back in his room. Logan bid him farewell, and left him to do his writing. Joshua sat at the desk and went to work:

Shoot the shot: The game-winning shot can never happen if you are afraid to shoot the ball In life, we have to at least try. The only thing worse than failure is wondering what could have happened if you had tried! The basket never made comes from the shot never taken.

Josh took the note, folded it, put it in an envelope and left it on the desk, then went to sleep. While he slept, another angel came in the room and took the envelope.

DAY 4

When Josh awoke, he decided to open the door to his room so that he could take a look around. To his surprise, outside of his room was the hallway of the hospital that his body had been taken to. Intrigued, he stepped into the hall and began to walk down the corridor. He found the hospital room where he was being kept and went in. By his bedside were Tiffany and Miranda. His room was filled with flowers and cards, but the thing that he loved most in the room was the picture that Miranda had drawn for him. She was the younger of the two girls, and she insisted that she and Tiffany spend every spare moment that they had at the hospital with their dad.

While they were in the room, Dr. Elkordy came in to check his vital signs. There was something oddly familiar about the hospital room, but Josh could not put his finger on what it was. Soon he realized that the surgery had already been done. He was still alive, but he was in a coma. The procedure had gone off without a hitch. He knew that Dr. Elkordy was the best person for the job, and she proved that by completing the procedure in an hour less than the other experts had expected. He was happy to see her in the room, and he wished that he could speak with her. Dr. Elkordy was very encouraging toward the children and they seemed to love her.

"Is my Daddy going to wake up soon?" Miranda asked.

"That's what we're hoping for," Dr. Elkordy replied.

"Can he hear us?" asked Tiffany.

"I think that he can," the doctor said, "so keep telling him how much you love him and how you can't wait for him to wake up so that you all can have fun together again."

"Daddy," Miranda said with tears in her eyes as she grabbed Josh's limp hand, "if you can hear me... I... I love you, and I want you to wake up so that you can play with me and help me with my homework, and pick me up from school so that we can eat pancakes before you drop me off with Mommy."

Miranda was only 5 years old when all of this took place. Despite her age, she was very aware of everything that was going on. Josh, the ghost-like version, was watching all of this. Tears welled up in his eyes as he watched his daughters talk to him. That's when Logan arrived.

"Are you ready to go, Josh?" Logan asked.

"I didn't know that they would be here. This must be so hard for them," Josh whispered, as he tried to choke back the tears.

"They only go home to change clothes and shower," Logan informed him.

"I love them so much. OK, where are you taking me today?" Josh inquired.

As usual, the scenery changed in the blink of an eye. Josh found himself in the office building of his first internship when he was in college. The college version of Josh walked into the room. He was not as confident as the Josh of later years. He sat at his desk and began to do his work. Several of the executives of the company walked in while conversing about a major deal that they were negotiating. He was amazed at the group of men and women. They all seemed to be so powerful and polished. One of them actually took the time to acknowledge Josh and invited him to come to lunch with them. He didn't feel worthy, and it came across in his conversation.

"I'm sorry sir," the younger Josh explained, "I'm just an intern."

"Listen kid, the only way that you will learn what you need to learn is by doing your best to get around the people who have exactly what you want. This is your shot... take it!" the young executive said. "And if you are going to make it in this world, you have to have a good reference group!"

"What's a reference group?" young Josh asked.

"Your reference group is the five people that you hang around the most," the young executive explained.

That was the day Josh learned a very important lesson. He told Logan that he was ready to go. Upon arriving in his room, he sat at his desk and began to write:

Surround yourself with good people: Proverbs 27:17 says, "As iron sharpens iron, so one man sharpens another" (NIV). Successful people understand that they are the average of the five people they hang around the most. Remember that people can be likened to the buttons on an elevator. They can either take you up, or take you down. Make sure that you surround yourself with people who will make your life better; and that you can help make their life better as well.

Josh took the note, folded it, put it in an envelope and left it on the desk, then went to sleep. While he slept, another angel came in the room and took the envelope.

DAY 5

Logan got to Josh's room before he was awake. Upon his arrival, Josh hopped up and prepared for the voyage of the day. There was no major conversation between the two of them before they left. Just a casual greeting, and they were on their way. Instantly, they were back at the hospital and Josh didn't know why.

"I thought we were going to learn another lesson. Why are we back where we started yesterday?" Josh asked as he followed Logan down the hall.

"Who said that we were where we were yesterday?" replied Logan.

"Um, it's the same hospital that my body is in. I know it when I see it," answered Josh in a smart-aleck tone.

"Um, how long have you been doing my job, 'Mr. I'm Josh-the-King-of-time-travel'?" Logan said in a mimicry voice.

They came to what Josh believed was the room that his body was in, and when the door opened Josh saw his uncle Moses in a hospital bed, hooked up to a life support machine. Josh's father Abraham was in a chair on the side of the bed holding his head in his hands with tears in his eyes. It was the exact same room that Josh saw his daughters in the day before, but the time period was different. This explained the "oddly familiar" feeling that Josh had felt the day before as well. It was the day that his uncle Moses had been injured in a diving accident. He was part of the Coast Guard, and he had an equipment malfunction while on a deep diving mission in Lake Michigan. Because of the malfunction, he was without air for nearly 15 minutes, and was in a coma. Only 7 years old at the time of the accident, Josh's mom Sarah escorted young Joshua into the room.

"I'm sorry, Moses," Abraham said as he choked back tears. "I'm sorry that this had to happen to you, and I'm sorry that we haven't spoken in six months." Prior to the accident, Abraham and Moses had an argument over a potential business deal. Both of them were too stubborn to deal with the matter, and unfortunately Abraham would never get a chance to hear Moses reply to his apology.

The older Josh sat in the corner with Logan watching the whole event play out. Even though he was only 7 at the time, he was old enough to understand what was going on. He also understood the pain that his father was going through. He gave the signal to Logan that he was ready to go. As a child, he was in the hospital room when Moses made the transition to the afterlife, and he didn't want to witness it again.

Once they got back to Josh's room, he asked Logan, "So did you take my Uncle Moses on the same journey that I'm going on?" **Logan informed him that not everyone gets to take this journey.** But he assured him that Moses made it into heaven. Josh went to his desk and wrote the following:

Say "I love you" before it's too late: We often take for granted the family and friends we have around us. We don't know how much time we will have to spend with them, so make sure that you let the people you love know that you love them. It can be the one thing that they needed to hear to really make their day! How would you feel if one of your loved ones had a tragic accident, and you didn't get a chance to tell them that you loved them? When the opportunity presents itself, say three of the most powerful words ever known to mankind... "I love you."

Josh took the note, folded it, put it in an envelope and left it on the desk, then went to sleep. While he slept, another angel came in the room and took the envelope.

DAY 6

"The early bird gets the worm! Wow! I'm starting to sound like Logan," Joshua said to himself as he got up for another day of time travel. A few sit-ups and a few push-ups to get the blood pumping was just what he needed. But on this day Josh noticed something that he hadn't really paid attention to for the past few days. Just as he was about to pose a question to himself, Logan walked in. Josh vocalized his concerns to his angel friend.

"Um, Logan... yeah, um... I've been here for almost what seems to be a week. Um, where the heck is the shower? The funny thing is... I don't smell bad."

Logan laughed as he replied to Josh's inquiry, saying, "Your body as you see it right now is not your physical body. You haven't had any food either, nor have you had to change clothes. Space and time as you normally experience them on earth are not the same in this realm."

"So, why do I sleep?" Josh asked.

"Well, you're not dead, but you're not alive. You're kind of in between. So you still need rest, especially for all the time traveling we do. Now, are you ready for the next..." and before Logan could say "trip" they were at the home that Josh grew up in. It was during Josh's freshman year in college, and his brother Donavan was in high school. "I'm still not done talking about the no-shower thing!" Josh told Logan as he glanced around his old house. Younger Josh had just gotten home for Thanksgiving break.

Donavan and Josh, the youthful versions, were sitting at the kitchen table talking. Donavan was on the debate team in high school. Not only did their parents push them to be great athletes, they also pushed them to be involved in mind-stimulating activities. Donavan had a disappointed look on his face as he sat there talking to Josh. His high school team had just lost a debate against their arch rivals, and Donavan felt like it was his fault. He had studied his subject matter, he knew his techniques, but he felt like he messed up at a crucial point in the debate.

"I could have done better, Josh," Donavan was explaining.

"I'm sure you gave them everything you had, D. You're a great debater," Josh replied.

"I had them on the ropes. I know that I was in the zone, and for some reason I went blank," said Donavan.

"You're one of the smartest guys on the team. Everybody has rough moments every now and then. It'll be OK," Josh said, trying to ease his younger brother's pain.

"It's not OK, Josh! I am one of the smartest people on the team, and I am expected to perform at my peak potential every debate. I went blank against Woodland College Prep! Do you know how long I will have to hear about this?!" Donavan exclaimed.

At that point in the conversation, their father walked in from work. He was the foreman at the iron plant just outside of Chicago. He wasn't a man of many words, but he had an undying love for his family. With the money that he made from the plant, he invested in other businesses so that he could provide a better life than he had for his two sons and his wife. When he did have something to say, it was usually simple, but profound.

"Welcome home, Joshua," Abraham said as he put his house keys on the kitchen counter.

"Thanks Pop, how was work?" Josh asked.

"Hello Donavan. Why do you look like your puppy just ran away? Work was fine, Josh," their father replied.

"I don't have a puppy Dad, and you would look like this too if you just botched the entire debate against your nemesis!" Donavan said.

"It couldn't have been that bad," laughed Abraham.

"I tried to tell him that Pop," Josh chimed in.

"It was worse than 'that bad.' This has got to be the most horrible moment in my debating career. I hope no college scouts were there. Oh my God... what if there were scouts there? What if I become a bum on the streets because nobody will accept me into their program? What if..." Donavan was rambling on when his father interrupted.

"What if you stop beating yourself up? Your mom and I didn't raise you to spaz out like this. Yes, we want you to strive for the best in everything that you do, but we don't want you to kill yourself in the process. There are enough people out there that don't want you to succeed. Let them handle the 'Anti-Donavan' campaign. You just focus on the future. So stop beating yourself up. You didn't die as a result of your actions, so that means that you can fight another day!" Abraham said.

Donavan sat and thought about what his dad told him. It made perfect sense, and he felt better about the debate. "Thanks dad. That kinda makes sense," Donavan said to his dad as he cleared his notebooks from the kitchen table and went to his room. Josh, the current spirit-like version told Logan that he was ready to go. When he arrived at his room, he went to his desk so that he could write down the lesson for the day. But before he started writing, he said to Logan "Don't think I forgot about the shower thing!" See you in the morning, or whatever it is when you come to take me on the next trip."

Josh began to write:

Don't beat yourself up... too many other people want to already: Don't be too hard on yourself. You can hold yourself to high standards without going overboard. There are enough opposing forces in the world that are against you, so there is no need to add yourself to the list of your enemies. How silly would it be to see a boxer punch himself in the face and stomach in between rounds? Why would he inflict pain on himself? His opponent already punches him enough. The same goes for you. Don't beat yourself up when the world wants to do it for you. Instead of beating yourself up, beat up the adversity that comes your way!

Josh took the note, folded it, put it in an envelope and left it on the desk, then went to sleep. While he slept, another angel came in the room and took the envelope.

DAY 7

When Josh awoke, he stayed in bed looking up at the ceiling. He was thinking about all that he had learned that past week, and how so many of the things that he applied in his life were not learned in the classroom. He was a well-educated man, but he was starting to realize that much of his knowledge could not be attributed to book knowledge. Instead, many of the little important things that he understood about life were learned during his daily interactions with people that he loved and respected… and as he would soon find out, some lessons came from people that he didn't like at all.

"Well, well, well! Looks like you've been up for a while Stokes," Logan said as he entered Josh's room with a huge smile on his face.

"And why do you look so happy today Angel Guy?" Josh asked.

"Joshua my friend, if you love what you do, you will never work a day in your life!" Logan exclaimed.

"So you love keeping people hostage in little rooms at night while you fly around the universe doing who knows what just so you can come and get them the next day and jump through…" and before Josh could say 'time' they were standing on the 50-yard-line of a football field.

"Yes," Logan laughed, "I do love it!"

The smell of fresh cut grass filled the air. The morning dew glistened on each blade of grass, adding to the brilliance of its emerald color. The white chalked lines were perfectly drawn on the field as if the king of geometry had done them himself! Josh remembered this day all too well. It was the first day of football camp right before his junior year in high school. For his first two years, Josh was on the offensive side of the ball. He was a great receiver. He was fast and alert on the field. The team was losing two very good players on the defensive side of the ball this year. Both of the corner backs had graduated and went on to play college ball. Josh and Logan watched as the high school football team marched to the field from the locker room.

"There I am, Logan!" Josh said with excitement as he pointed to number 38 jogging with his helmet in his hand. "This is my high school football camp!"

"You look the same now as you did back then, except for a few sprinkles of gray hair," Logan replied.

It sounded like a low thunder as the team went by Josh and Logan. The kids were excited and looking forward to a great season, even though they didn't make the play-offs the year before. Several key players were injured, but the head coach remained optimistic. His name was Coach Valor, and he had coached several years of college football. He was brought in by the athletic director of Leonidis High School—the school that Josh attended—to turn their football program around and make them a winning team again. The players were getting ready for warm- ups when a season altering conversation took place.

"Stokes." Coach Valor called for Josh.

"Yes sir?" Josh replied as he ran in the head coach's direction.

"You're being moved to defense. We lost Giandonato and Yoder last year, so we need somebody fast to play Corner. I believe in you Stokes, but I need to know if you think you can handle it?" Valor explained.

"Whatever you think is best, sir. I will give it everything I've got," Josh said.

Josh eagerly ran toward the defensive back coach to report for duty. Coach Celoso had played a few years in the NFL, and he thought that he should have been named head coach instead of Coach Valor. He knew the game well, but his attitude was not the best. He wasn't excited about Josh being moved to the defense. Actually, he wasn't really excited about anything.

"I've been moved to defense, sir," Josh said when he got to Coach Celoso.

"Don't you think I know that already. I'm a coach," Celoso replied.

Josh began to make his way toward the rest of the defensive backs when he heard, "Did I tell you to move? Since you think you call the shots, give me 20 stadium striders!"

A "stadium strider" is when players have to run up and down the steps of the stadium all the way to the top, then back down. Up and down once is one stadium strider. "Yes sir," Josh said as he headed toward his daunting task.

The older Josh said to Logan, "That guy tried to kill me that year."

"Obviously you survived," replied Logan.

"Yeah, but I didn't like it," Josh said with a slight frown on his face as they looked on.

The younger Joshua finished his stadium striders, and was running toward his defensive teammates when he heard, "Stokes!" being yelled at him from Coach Celoso. He immediately changed directions to see what Celoso wanted.

"Yes sir?" Josh inquired as he approached his new coach.

"I don't think that you are in good enough condition to play on my defense yet. My players are strong, and you don't look the part. Go play catch with the sled to get your stomach in shape. Three sets of 100 should do."

Sled catch was not a "fun" activity. It's when a player has to do sit-ups with a 15-pound medicine ball, bounce the ball off the sled at the top of the sit-up (a device used for hitting drills), catch the medicine ball, and go back to the horizontal position in the sit-up exercise. Celoso knew that Joshua was one of Valor's favorite players. The only reason that Josh was getting this unfair treatment was because of Celoso's jealousy of Coach Valor. Josh didn't even really practice with the team at all that day. He just went through exercise after exercise as he was instructed to do.

"If I went to kick him right now, would he feel it Logan?" the older Josh asked.

"No," Logan said with a laugh.

"Why was he so hard on me? I never did anything to the guy!" said Josh.

"How did the team do that year?" asked Logan.

"We actually were the State Champs!" Josh remembered and said with a smile.

"And how was your performance that season?"

"Incredible, actually. I was in several newspapers, and led the team in interceptions."

"Really?" Logan said. "So why did you dislike Celoso so much?"

"He disliked me… and he hated Coach Valor even more. He took it out on me."

"But were you a better player because of him?"

"I don't know how to answer that."

"That which doesn't kill you may actually give you strength."

"I see what you mean. I was too wrapped up in my dislike for him to get this lesson on my own. Thanks, Logan. Can we go now?"

"You don't want to see the part where you barf from doing too much exercise?" Logan asked.

The look on Josh's face let Logan know that he wasn't amused. When Josh got back to his room, he sat at the desk and began to write:

Be persistent in the face of resistance: Resistance is not necessarily a bad thing. In order for an airplane to achieve lift during take-off, it needs wind resistance. In other words, it goes against the wind to achieve its goal. In weight lifting, the negative resistance is what helps you build muscle. Once your muscles are able to handle a certain amount of negative resistance, you are able to lift more! You get stronger! The same principles apply in life. When you are able to overcome resistance, you get stronger! Remember... No struggle, no progress!

Josh took the note, folded it, put it in an envelope and left it on the desk, then went to sleep. While he slept, another angel came in the room and took the envelope.

~~

Hey reader! Yes, I'm talking to you again. Are you enjoying the voyage so far? Congrats on making it to this point! Did you know that most people don't even read books after high school? You are an amazing human being! Are you reading straight through, or are you reading one lesson per day? Either way, I'd like to commend you for your stick ability! That means your ability to stick with something until it is complete. Don't pat yourself on the back too much though. This is only the first week in Josh and Logan's adventures. You've made it through Book 1, but Book 2 has some great lessons in it as well. Are you going to hang out with us some more, or are you going to be a quitter and not make it through the rest of the story? The choice is yours! Hopefully, we will meet again!

BOOK 2

Welcome to Book 2! I'm so glad that you decided to continue on. That little voice in your head is probably saying, "How is he talking to me from a book... and wait, what little voice is he talking about?" That little voice right there... that's the one I was talking about. Don't worry about that right now though. You have more reading to do! Joshua Stokes is able to survive because you haven't given up. His existence is based on your co-existence with this book. So buckle up and get ready for more of this wonderful adventure!

DAY 8

On the first day of the second week of this miraculous journey, Josh was awakened by the warmth of the sun coming through the window of his room. He never noticed a window before. As a matter of fact, he had explored every nook and cranny of the room and there was no window to be found before. He jumped up in amazement, rushing toward the window to see what he could see. It overlooked a beautiful garden filled with the bright colors of fruits, vegetables, and flowers. Now even more piqued by his curiosity, Josh ran toward the door of the room to see what was on the outside of it. There was only one door, and he remembered opening it before only to find "outer-space-like" scenery. Slowly turning the knob as far as it would go, he yanked the door open. The entrance/exit way to his room had not altered at all. Josh closed the door and went back to look out of the window. The garden was still there, and the sun was still shining. He went back to the door to open it again. When he pulled it open, Logan was standing in the doorway. Josh recognized that the outside of his room was now the inside of the hospital.

"I'm not even going to ask how you just did that," Josh said.

"Did what?"

"The whole door thing, not to mention installing a window in my room while I was asleep."

"Well, do you like it?"

"How would you feel if you were in a room like this and stuff changed without warning, and you were hungry? Wait! I'm hungry!" Josh said as he grabbed Logan by the shoulders.

"Ahh yes, hungry. I was hoping this wouldn't happen so soon," Logan said with a slight look of disappointment.

"Why, Logan? Is something wrong with me?" Josh inquired.

"I wouldn't say wrong..." Logan signaled for Josh to walk with him out of the room and down the hall of the hospital. "It's just part of your healing process. Your spirit form is reconnecting with your physical form."

"So what exactly does that mean?"

"Basically, you're a step closer to either living or dying," Logan explained.

"So do I go meet God now or something?" Josh asked with a puzzled look on his face.

"Joshua, the journey of a million miles starts with a single step. This is just one step in the process. And remember, you will either live or die. Nothing is etched in stone right now."

The two gentlemen, well the gentleman and the angel, made their way down the hall toward the hospital room where Josh's body was being kept. Upon entering, Josh saw the nurse putting something into his feeding tubes. Since his physical form was still unconscious, he was on a liquid diet. Josh walked over to the nurse to get a closer look at what she was giving him. He read the contents of the meal about to be injected into his feeding bag. One of the ingredients was beef extract.

"Stop!" Josh yelled at the nurse. Everything in the room stopped just like it did at the bank.

"What just happened, Logan?" Josh said looking around the room.

"You said 'Stop,' and it stopped," replied Logan.

"I thought I could only do that with past events. You're confusing me."

"This is a past event, Josh. This is two days after your surgery."

"I don't remember any of this. How am I to learn a lesson from something I wasn't conscious for?" asked Josh.

"Un-pause time and let's find out," Logan instructed.

Josh did just that, and the nurse was getting ready to administer his meal when Dr. Elkordy walked into the room and yelled, "Stop! What are you about to give him? If he was awake he would have a heart attack. Joshua Stokes is a vegetarian, and he does not eat meat at all... even if he is in a coma," she said.

"You look relieved," Logan said to Josh.

"I sure am. I haven't eaten meat in years."

"That may be one of the reasons why your recovery is going so well."

"What do you mean?"

"Rest, diet, and exercise are essential to health and well being." Logan explained.

"That makes sense."

"So your diet..." Logan started to say, as Josh interrupted.

"Take me back to my room please, Logan. I want to write this one before I forget."

Seconds later, Josh was back in his room. They didn't even walk back down the hall to get there. Josh was somewhat used to this method of travel, and it didn't surprise him at all. He rushed to the desk, said goodbye to Logan, and began to write:

Don't dig your grave with your teeth: Most people underestimate the importance of a good diet. The old saying that "an apple a day keeps the doctor away" shows that a consistent diet is important. You can't wait until your health is bad and try to eat 1,000 apples to catch up on what you missed. What you eat can help you live longer, or help you die faster. Figure out a balanced diet so that you can live long and be happy with plenty of energy.

Josh took the note, folded it, put it in an envelope and left it on the desk, then went to sleep. While he slept, another angel came in the room and took the envelope.

DAY 9

Josh woke up to the smell of an enticing breakfast. French toast, an array of colorful fruits, and even vegetarian breakfast sausage! He could hardly believe his eyes, let alone his stomach. Logan walked in just as Josh was starting to indulge in the feast that was before him.

"I was going to ask you about the hunger thing when you got here, but I see you handled it," Josh said with a tone of thanks in his voice.

"I didn't do anything. It was my angel friend Annapurna," Logan explained.

"Wait, wait, wait! You've got to be kidding me."

"Kidding about what?"

"Annapurna, like the Hindu goddess of food?"

"You say goddess, I know her as an angel," Logan stated.

"I went to a Catholic high school, but I learned about her in a 'World Religion' class that I…"

Josh was mid-sentence when the entire scenery changed. He and Logan were now in the very class that he was speaking of.

"Stop doing that! I wasn't finished eating either!" he complained.

"We still have a lot of work to do, Josh," Logan said as he signaled Josh to pay attention to what was about to happen.

Students were filing into the room and taking their seats as Josh and Logan looked on. Mr. Johnson, Josh's religion teacher, was sitting at the desk greeting the students as they walked in. There was something different about Mr. Johnson on this day. He had missed the past week of school, and the students knew that he had been in the hospital. As soon as the class settled down, Mr. Johnson stood up to speak to his students.

"Hello class, it's good to see you all again," Mr. Johnson said.

"Welcome back, Mr. Johnson," one of the students said.

"We're glad you're back, sir. The substitute wasn't as fun as you are," another added.

"Thanks. I'm glad to be back. I need to share something with you guys."

"Hopefully not a pop quiz," said Allen Louis, the class clown.

"No, this is even more serious than a pop quiz. I'm not going to finish teaching the rest of the school year. I've been diagnosed with terminal cancer," Mr. Johnson explained.

An awkward hush fell over the room as the students looked at Mr. Johnson, some with tears filling up their eyes.

"It's going to be OK," Mr. Johnson went on, "I just need to take some time to heal myself."

"Heal yourself? How are you going to do that?" one student inquired.

"I thought that people always died when they had cancer?" another student added.

"Well, I don't believe that I have to die just because I have the disease," Johnson explained.

"But you're a teacher, not a doctor. How can you not die if they said you would?" the younger Joshua asked.

"Josh," said Johnson, "I only tell myself the things that I want to manifest in my life. Just because somebody else said that cancer was going to get the best of me, I don't have to believe them. I'm going to focus on living, so therefore I will live!" Mr. Johnson said with absolute certainty.

The students looked at Mr. Johnson in a puzzled fashion. He was talking about healing himself from a disease that was determined by doctors to be fatal. This went against the normal way of thinking. If the doctors were the experts, how could he do something that was contrary to what they told him? Was it possible for him to defy the odds and actually heal himself? The conversation went on between Mr. Johnson and the class while Josh and Logan watched.

"Logan, I remember this conversation very well. Mr. Johnson was a great teacher," said Josh.

"Do you remember what happened to him, Josh?"

"Yes, I do. He didn't finish the school year. He didn't even return to teaching while I was still in high school. But while I was in college, he started teaching again. He actually beat the cancer and lived a great life." With a smile on his face, Josh said, "I'm ready to go now."

When he got back to his room, Josh wrote:

Only plant the seeds that you want to grow: If a farmer wants to grow corn, he or she will not plant cabbage where they want the corn to grow. You get what you plant in life. If you have a specific goal in mind, only plant the things that will help that goal grow! An apple tree doesn't bare oranges. The same goes for the tree of your life. Only plant what you want to grow.

Josh took the note, folded it, put it in an envelope and left it on the desk, then went to sleep. While he slept, another angel came in the room and took the envelope.

DAY 10

Josh woke up on Day 10 to the same spread that was there the day before. He thought to himself that he was not going to let Logan ruin it for him this day. Josh ate as much food as he could as fast as possible. Logan arrived and found Josh looking like a chipmunk with enlarged cheeks full of food.

"If you could see yourself right now," Logan said with a laugh.

"I'm just trying to make sure I get a meal in before you 'alacazam' me into another world," Josh said, sounding muffled with a mouth full of food.

Just as Josh expected, they were whisked off into another world before he could blink. This time, Logan took him to Tiffany's room at Josh's house where they lived while he was still married. Tiffany was the older of the two girls, and she was in her freshman year of high school during the time period that Logan transported Josh to. At the time, she was the only freshman to make the varsity cheerleading team. She was totally excited, and her parents were excited for her. The only challenge was that she began to hang around older students who didn't have the kind of habits that Josh wanted his children to develop. Josh and Logan watched as the story began to unfold. Tiffany was talking on the phone sitting on the side of her bed.

"You heard that Trina was the reason that Renee didn't make the team?" Tiffany said.

"And Jacky told you what?!" Tiffany continued, her voice sounding rather annoyed.

She was talking to one of the other girls on the cheerleading team. The conversation went on for a few minutes, and it was apparent that Tiffany was becoming uncomfortable with the topic of discussion. Her body language said it all. First she was sitting on the side of the bed. Then she was lying in the bed staring at the ceiling fan. Eventually she wound up on the floor rolling around in mock pain from what she was hearing.

"Listen Dianna, I can't be a part of this conversation anymore, it's giving me a headache!" Just as Tiffany was hanging up the phone, her father was knocking at her door.

"Scooch, you finished with your homework?" Josh asked from the other side of the door.

"Not yet dad. Come in for a minute please," she replied.

"What's up kiddo? Are you OK?"

"Yeah, kinda," Tiffany said.

"Is it something that you want to talk about? Or am I no longer the 'cool' parent that you used to tell everything?" Josh asked.

"You're still the cool parent," Tiffany laughed. "I just had to hang up on Dianna."

"Is there a civil war among the cheerleaders?" he asked.

"Not really. She was just being really negative. I'm not a fan of gossip dad," she replied.

"Wow Scooch, I'm proud of you. I thought all teenagers like gossip," Josh said.

"Nooo! You taught me better than that. Gossip is like garbage, they both stink!" Tiffany exclaimed.

"My little Scooch is growing up!" Josh smiled.

"Yes, I am dad, and please make sure you don't call me 'Scooch' in front of my friends," Tiffany begged.

Josh gave his oldest daughter a big hug and a kiss on the forehead before he left the room. As he began to walk down the stairs toward the main level of the house, his cell phone rang. It was one of his business partners. Logan and the hospitalized-spirit-like Josh followed him down the stairs. They could see the look of disgust on his face as he listened to the gentleman on the other end of the phone line. After about 30 seconds into the conversation, Josh interrupted his partner.

"Rodrick, I can't do this conversation right now. Gossip is like garbage, both of them stink. Either be part of the problem or part of the solution. Thanks for the call, but I'm sure you can figure out what to do without the negativity. You're still my friend, but you need to handle this situation a little better. Call me in the morning and let me know what you came up with."

Josh hung up the phone, and Logan and spirit-Josh were suddenly back in Josh's room where his desk and paper were. Oddly enough, Josh didn't even question Logan as to why they left before Logan was notified that he was ready to go. He just went to his desk and began to write. There was a smile on his face that stretched from ear to ear.

"You look happy," Logan said to Josh.

"Yep! I sure am!" Josh continued to smile.

"I'll be back to get you for another adventure tomorrow," said Logan as he left the room.

Josh began to write:

Gossip is like garbage, both of them stink: There is no reason to gossip. Talking about other people is not part of your success plan. If you are not conversing with the person the situation involves, or if you are not trying to help figure out how to solve a particular problem, there is no need to talk about it at all. Too many people get wrapped up in issues that do not concern them. All too often the situation becomes more of a mess because of people gossiping about it. The person that gossips has a garbage truck for a mouth.

Josh took the note, folded it, put it in an envelope and left it on the desk, then went to sleep. While he slept, another angel came in the room and took the envelope.

DAY 11

When Josh woke up, he just stayed in bed smiling. He couldn't stop thinking of how proud he was of his daughter. There was food in the room, but Josh didn't even touch it. Surprisingly, he didn't even get up to exercise like he normally did. He just sat in bed remembering different events about his children. If you could see his face, you would know how happy he was.

"Children are great, aren't they?" Logan said, startling Josh.

"If I wasn't so happy right now, I'd complain about my privacy and lack of a locking door."

"You were such a positive person on earth. Why so touchy now?" Logan asked.

"Hmmm, let me see. I got shot in the head, kidnapped by an angel, and I sleep in a room where food magically appears. Didn't we have this conversation before?"

"But is the food good?"

"Can I switch tour guides? You're not my favorite right now."

"Let's talk about that after today's journey," Logan said with a laugh.

Josh hopped out of bed, grabbed an apple off of the serving tray, and waited for Logan to do his magic. As expected, Josh found himself out of his room and in a new environment. This time he was back on the campus where he went to college. Josh saw a younger version of himself walking into the university library. He spent a lot of time there because it was often too noisy to study at the fraternity house where he lived.

"This has to be about my junior year in college," Josh said to Logan.

"Those were the good old days," Logan laughed.

"You say that like you remember 'the good old days' - as if you went to college," Josh inquired.

"You think time travel is easy? I had years of rigorous training to learn this stuff," Logan explained.

They followed college-Josh into the library to see what the lesson of the day would be. The place was crowded. Students were getting ready for semester exams, and it seemed as if the library was some sort of Mecca for those who wanted to study hard. The only spot that the younger Josh saw available was a two-seater table where a young lady with glasses was already sitting. Even though Josh was a social butterfly in college, he really didn't like sitting with other people when he was studying. Especially when he was studying Latin! It was one of the toughest classes of his entire college career.

"Is this seat taken?" Josh asked the young lady.

"Not really, but I… never mind," she replied.

"Never mind what? I'm not trying to ask for a date. I just need to study."

"I just like studying by myself, but you can sit here. By the way, I don't date frat boys."

"Well I like to study alone too, but there are no seats. It's exam week. Thanks," said Josh.

Josh took his seat and pulled out what had to be the largest text book in the history of mankind. It was apparent that he was frustrated with the class by the sighs and moans that he let out as he studied. The wrinkles in his forehead deepened with every turn of the page. Josh loved a challenge, but with all of the other obligations he had at school Latin was a bit much. His frustration made it hard for him to sit still. Finally, the young lady interrupted Josh.

"Mr. Ants-in-Your-Pants, I'm trying to study," she said.

"The name is Josh, and I do apologize. I'm having a hard time," he said to her.

"And my name is Nicole, and what are you studying?" she asked.

"Latin unfortunately. I should just drop the ball. I'm going to fail," Josh said in a low voice.

"Frat boy taking Latin? Did you lose a bet or something?" she asked.

"There is more to me than being a 'frat boy' as you put it. No, I didn't lose a bet. By the way, my fraternity does a lot of community service."

"Well, I'll help you with your Latin, but it has to be on my terms," Nicole said.

"What makes you qualified to help me?" he asked.

"My dad is a Latin professor in Bermuda. I grew up learning Latin and three other languages," she answered.

"What are your terms?" he asked with a heightened curiosity.

"I really only have one rule, but it goes for every area of your life. This isn't just about Latin class," Nicole stated.

"Are you going to tell me or what?" Josh asked.

"If I agree to tutor you, you can't drop the class. In life, the only time you fail is when you quit. You don't strike me as the quitting type. I doubt that you ever give up on a challenge in sports or other things, so I need you to have that same attitude about this class," she stated.

"You're right. I give you my word that I won't drop the class."

"Facta non verba," Nicole responded.

"What does that mean?" he asked with a puzzled look on his face.

"Deeds, not words. Show me your commitment," Nicole demanded.

"So can the next study session be over dinner that you cook me?"

"I told you I don't date frat boys," Nicole said with a smile.

"I'm not trying to have a date! I'm trying to have a meal. Amor platonicus."

"Platonic love?" Nicole laughed.

"I haven't learned how to say 'just friends' yet," Josh laughed.

Logan and Josh watched as his younger self sat in the library with Nicole. This was one of the most memorable days of his college career. It was the day that he decided to take challenges head-on when he faced them. Nicole started a fire that would never be extinguished. Josh smiled as he watched the conversation. Logan noticed that there was a different look in his eyes.

"Are you OK, Josh?" Logan asked.

"Yes, I'm fine. I'm ready to head back when you are," Josh replied.

"No problem," said Logan.

Logan transported them back to Josh's room. Josh immediately went to his seat so that he could write down the lesson for the day.

"So how did you do in that Latin class?" Logan asked.

"I got an A-minus," Josh said.

"What ever happened to Nicole?" Logan continued.

"We wound up dating until we graduated from school. Now if you will excuse me, I have some writing to do."

Josh began to write:

You only fail if you quit: The only true failure comes with totally giving up. You may not get it on the first try, or even on the one millionth try, but you are not a failure until you quit. Giving up is the easiest thing to do, especially when times are hard. But the person that sticks with a task is a person that will never fail. Napoleon Hill once said, "Victory is always possible for the person who refuses to stop fighting." If you fall down seven times, just remember that you must get up and dust yourself off eight times.

Josh took the note, folded it, put it in an envelope and left it on the desk, then went to sleep. While he slept, another angel came in the room and took the envelope.

DAY 12

Day 12 started off magnificent. The window in Josh's room was open and a wonderful breeze was blowing through it. There was a breakfast spread fit for a king… well, a vegetarian king. Josh sat on the edge of the bed patiently awaiting Logan's arrival. He ate until his stomach could hold no more, but there was still no sign of Logan. Curious of his friend's location, Josh went to the door and opened it. The scenery was very familiar. The door of his room actually led to what appeared to be the front porch of his grandmother's house in Alabama. There he found Logan wearing a straw hat and sitting in a hand-carved rocking chair.

"Mornin' Josh," Logan said with a Southern accent.

"Um, good morning. Why are you talking like that?"

"I reckon' I should speak like the locals. We're fixin' ta have a good ole time today."

"Really Logan, you can stop now."

"Mighty fine day today, sir. Shol' feels like it's gonna' be a hot one though."

"OK, I see this isn't going to stop anytime soon. Why are we here?"

Right at that moment, two little boys came running onto the porch. It was Josh and Donavan when they were kids. Josh had to be around 11 years old and Donavan was about 9. They were out of breath, and excited about whatever it was they had just seen. Their eyes were bulging with enthusiasm. They had just come from the Monroe's house down the road.

"Grandma! Grandma!" they yelled as they ran up the steps.

"Yes babies?" Their grandmother Thelma appeared in the doorway with a pitcher of fresh lemonade.

"Kerry and Kenneth just got new fishing poles and they are going down to the creek to go fishing!" Donavan exclaimed.

"Well that's wonderful, Donnie," she said as she poured two glasses of lemonade for them.

"Can we go into town and get new fishing poles, granny?" asked Josh.

"Baby, your grandfather had to spend what extra money we had on fixin' the tractor. We can't buy you fishing poles this week. But if you don't have a horse, ride a mule," Thelma stated.

"We're not tryna' ride the mule granny. We just want to go fishing," Josh replied.

"No baby, I wasn't saying you should go ride Hank out by the barn. I meant that you have to learn to improvise," she said.

"How do we impernize?" asked Donavan.

"Not 'impernize' baby. Improvise. Use what you have access to. See that tree over there? Those branches can be used as poles. Your granddad has some fishing line in the shed, and since it rained yesterday I'm willin' to bet that there are earthworms wigglin' in the mud by the barn. You will have plenty of bait. The fishing poles you make will be able to out-catch any fancy lil pole that the Monroe boys have," Thelma said as the boys drank their lemonade.

Donavan and Josh looked at each other with big smiles. They ran to the tree and got some limber, yet strong branches. Their grandfather helped them attach the fishing line to the branches. They even found a box of fishing hooks in the shed that hadn't been used. Thelma brought an old jar from inside the house to give them for their worms. Twenty minutes later, the boys were running proudly toward the creek with their "new" fishing poles.

Logan looked over at Josh and said, "Yep. Mighty fine day indeed."

Josh laughed and said, "Yes sir, it is a mighty fine day. Reckon I'll be headin' to my room now."

Josh walked back through the door and sat at the desk so that he could write the lesson for the day:

When my grandmother was alive, she used to always have a saying when things didn't go as planned. She would say "If you don't have a horse, ride a mule." In other words, don't let yourself be stopped if the need to change your original plan arises. If you don't have exactly what you need, there may be a way for you to improvise and still get the job done.

Josh took the note, folded it, put it in an envelope and left it on the desk, then went to sleep. While he slept, another angel came in the room and took the envelope.

DAY 13

It had been 13 days since Josh's near fatal incident at the bank. The surgery was successful, but there still were no signs to the outside world that he would recover. Meanwhile, he had been traveling to past days of his life that were not at the forefront of his memory. This day was no different. Josh exercised and ate breakfast, then patiently waited for Logan's arrival. His intergalactic tour guide was taking longer than usual to show up. Josh had some extra time to think before Logan got there, and had a very important question he wanted to ask. Logan walked into the room and Josh asked his question before Logan could even speak.

"What happened to all the envelopes that I've put my letters in every night?" Josh asked.

"I don't know. I'm gone before you even finish writing. Good morning to you too by the way," Logan replied.

"Yeah yeah, top of the mornin' to you as well. I've written at least 10 notes and…"

"It's been 12," Logan interrupted. "Ready to go?" he asked.

"Dude, come on. You're telling me that you have no idea at all where my…"

"Josh, I take you places to review life lessons. That's my job and that's it," Logan explained.

"You work for God right? You know 'Thou shalt not lie' is one of the rules He put in place?" Josh said in a serious tone.

With a smile on his face, Logan snapped his fingers and changed the scenery. They were in a wooded area where there was a wooden fort that had plenty of windows and a look-out tower. The fort sat on top of a steep hill. It looked like it was a huge club house made by some very creative teenagers. What stood out most was the color of the fort... well, more like the colors of the fort. There were too many colors to name!

"I remember this place!" Josh exclaimed.

"You seem excited my friend," Logan said.

"This is where I first played the game of paintball," Josh stated as the sound of paintballs pelting the side of the fort started hailing from nowhere followed by loud yells.

About 30 young adults (15 on each team) were running up opposite sides of the hill that the fort sat on. "AAARRRRHHHH THUMP, THUMP, THUMP, THUMP, THUMP, THUMP, THUMP, THUMP" was all that could be heard as weekend warriors took their positions on the battlefield trying to gain ground and eliminate the enemy.

"There you are, Josh," Logan pointed to a 20-year-old kid toward the back of the Red Team on the east side of the hill.

"Yeah, I was a newbie," Josh said.

"You don't look like you are having much fun," Logan replied.

"I had no idea what I was doing. I saw a game of paintball on TV and thought it was a good idea to go try it," Josh explained

At that very moment, the young Joshua Stokes started running full speed toward the front line of the battle with his paintball marker pointed at the opposing team. He made it to a bunker that was close to the fort. There were four guys on the same team behind a bunker about 10 yards in front of him. In all the excitement, he accidently shot one of his own teammates in the back of the head while trying to shoot over the bunker at their foes. Wide-eyed and full of adrenalin, Josh charged toward the fort and was taken out in a matter of seconds. His clothes were covered with so much paint, it looked like he was the victim of a kindergarten finger painting project. After the round was over, the younger Josh was met on the side of the field by four guys. Josh and Logan watched from a distance.

"You're pretty fast!" one of the guys said.

"Yeah, but he has horrible aim. I don't mind getting shot, but I hate it when it comes from somebody that is supposed to be on my side!" said another guy.

"My deepest apologies," said Josh, "this is my first time playing."

"Never mind my brother, he would have gotten shot anyway. My name is Bear," said one guy.

"Bear? Um, okay... I'm Josh," stuttered the young Josh.

"Josh? What type of call sign is that? Anyway, that's my brother Deuces that you shot in the head, that's Elbows, and that's Danny Gunz." Bear said as he introduced the rest of the guys.

"You all have interesting nicknames," said Josh.

"CALL SIGNS!" Deuces exclaimed.

"Calm down Deuces, the kid is new to the sport," Bear jumped in.

"Stop being a baby Deuces, you're the oldest guy on our team," Elbows said with a laugh.

"Well Josh, we need to get you a call sign. The four of us always play together, and we've been looking for another guy to play with. We could use your speed, but you need a better name than 'Josh' if you're gonna' run with us. There is another guy on the team we call 'Spooner' but he doesn't get out much anymore," Bear said.

"How about Grease Lightning?" Danny Gunz suggested.

"How about 'He Shot Me In The Head'?" Deuces blurted.

"Man, quit crying!" the other three said in unison.

"How about Tom Slick!? Like the old cartoon race car driver!" Elbows suggested.

"Tom Slick has a decent ring to it, I guess." Josh said.

"Tom Slick it is!" said Bear.

"We play a lot, and we would be willing to show you the ropes if you like," Deuces said "as long as you don't shoot me again."

"Sure! This is all new to me, but I'm totally excited about the challenge of the game," Josh said.

"Well then, let's get this excess paint off of our gear and get ready for the next round! We gonna' go huntin' for the bad guys!" Danny Gunz said with a smile.

The five of them walked to a table where they cleaned up and reloaded. Josh and Logan stood there as the conversation continued. You could see the excitement in young Josh's face as he got to know his new friends. This was truly something that he was happy to take part in.

"Those guys became some very good friends," Josh told Logan.

"What made paintball so exciting for you?" Logan asked.

"It was new, fun, and the friends that I made were really good people. It was all new to me, and the challenge helped me grow. Once I was having fun and success in paintball, it started to spill over in other areas of my life. I never knew a game could do that. Can we go back to my jail cell… I mean room now, please?" Josh said with a smile.

"As you wish Tom Slick, King of Paintball Land!" Logan said as he snapped his fingers.

Josh sat at his desk and wrote:

Pick up a hobby that challenges you: When you do something fun, but challenging, it can help you build your confidence. The fact that it is fun will help you enjoy it. When it challenges you, it forces you to grow. That new confidence can be transferred to other areas of your life.

Josh took the note, folded it, put it in an envelope and left it on the desk, then went to sleep. While he slept, another angel came in the room and took the envelope.

DAY 14

Two weeks after the dreadful shooting at the bank, Josh is still in the hospital. The surgery is over, but nobody really knows if he is going to be OK. His daughters have spent every moment that they are not in school at the hospital. Josh isn't even sure himself as to what his fate will be. What he does know is that he has been able to see some distant memories that showed him the moments in his life that shaped his character. Did he miss his children? Without question! Were there people that he had unfinished business within the "conscious" world? Undoubtedly, but for right now, all he can do is take things one lesson at a time.

Josh slept in on this day. There was no breakfast or exercise activities before Logan arrived for the voyage of the day. Josh was very hungry, but he didn't eat. All he could do was lay there thinking about the people he loved. This experience made him realize that he had some very cool friends, and family members that he missed deeply. As usual, Logan arrived and was ready to get the lesson for the day underway.

"Greetings and salutations, Mr. Stokes! You ready to rock?" Logan greeted Josh.

"Is there any way that we can speed things along Logan? I really want to get back to my kids," Josh said.

"I can't promise you that you will live Josh. I told you at the beginning that your recovery would take some time, and at the end of all of this you will have to make a decision. I did not tell you what that decision will be," Logan explained.

"Look, I just want to get this over with, and…"

Before Josh could finish his sentence, Logan transported them back to the hospital. Josh was still in a coma, and there was a tube attached to his head that was draining excess fluid from his brain. Standing over his bed stood Vanessa. She had the elegance of a dancer even in street clothes. Her eyes were red from crying, and her hair was in a pony tail. By her appearance, you could tell that she hadn't had much sleep. She began to speak to Josh, her voice cracking with every sentence.

"Josh, I don't know if you can hear me. I guess part of me hopes that you can't. I don't want to put you in any more pain than you are already in. I know you are wondering why I haven't been here to visit you until now. I wish that I could come up with a better answer than the one I am about to give you. The truth of the matter is I was looking for an easy way out for a long time now. I don't know if I can handle being with you. I'm just a dance teacher and you... well you are Mr. Popular. I didn't know how to tell you this before. I'm moving to Europe. Life will be easier for me there. I can start over and try to... to... I don't know. I don't want you to think that I don't love you. I really do. It's just that... I just... goodbye Josh." She left a single white rose on the table next to his bed, kissed him on the cheek, and walked out of the room.

A single tear rolled down Josh's cheek. Not only the spirit-Josh, but the Josh in the hospital bed as well. Logan was very uncomfortable. He wanted to say something to Josh, but he couldn't find the words. Josh stood there in amazement. He really didn't know what to say either. Part of him was upset that Vanessa picked now, of all times, to walk out on him. The other part of him was very understanding. He was a little older than she was, and they didn't see eye to eye on everything. They were great friends, but apparently they wanted different things when it came to their romantic relationship. When Josh and Logan finally looked at each other, Logan knew that it was time to go.

Upon their return, Josh went right to his desk and wrote:

When you truly love someone, all that you want is for them to be happy. That means that you want them to be happy even if it means they will not be with you. The people you care about may not always be around when you think you need them most. Our first impulse is to be mad at them. The reality of it all is that we don't know what they are going through. Everybody does not have the same capacity to love. You have to know that you can make it through anything as long as you know the love of God can get you through anything.

Josh took the note, folded it, put it in an envelope and left it on the desk, then went to sleep. While he slept, another angel came in the room and took the envelope.

~~

Well, that was different huh? I wasn't expecting that, were you? Don't be mad at Vanessa. People deal with events differently. She only did what she knew how to do. Josh didn't get all bent out of shape about it, so you shouldn't either. Besides, the most important thing is his recovery right now. It's tough when people desert you while you're down and out. Guess what though… those are the times when you have to develop the inner strength necessary to carry on. If Josh can do it, so can you. Speaking of Josh, I wonder what happens to him next. I guess there is only one real way to find out. I hope you don't give up on him now. I have a feeling things are about to get really interesting!

BOOK 3

Hey! You made it half way through the story. WOW, I have to congratulate you. Paul J. Meyer once said "Ninety percent of the people who fail in life are not defeated, they simply give up." It doesn't matter if you are the type of person who looks at the cup as half empty or half full… you are HALFWAY TO THE END! So, are you going to be part of the 90 percent that fail because they give up? Or are you going to press forward and join Josh for the rest of his journey? Why am I asking you this? I already know you're not a quitter or else you would not have come this far. Let's see what lessons await Josh in this third week of his journey…

DAY 15

Two weeks and a couple of angels into his voyage, Josh woke up early and excited about what was to come in the start of his third week of time travel. As expected, the food was there for him to eat. He knew that breakfast was the most important meal of the day, so he ate until his heart and his stomach were content. After his meal, he went to sit at his desk where he noticed a small picture frame with a photograph of Tiffany and Miranda in it. This made Josh smile, but he really missed his children. While he was gazing at the picture, Logan walked in.

"Good morning, Josh."

"Hey Wolverine… I mean Logan," Josh said with a smile.

"Well, you seem to be in a good mood this morning," Logan replied.

"I am, and thanks for bringing this picture of my girls from my desk at home while I was sleeping."

"Oh, that wasn't me Josh... you did that yourself," Logan said.

"Huh? What do you mean, I did it? It's not like there is a Walmart outside my door." Josh replied.

"OK, how can I explain this to you? Um... see you have the ability to bring things into existence by thinking about them. You have that ability on earth, but..."

"Wait a minute, man! You are telling me that I thought this up?" asked Josh.

"On earth, there is a slight delay in manifesting what you think about. But here, it can be almost instant once you master it. But yes, you were thinking about the picture you had on your desk back home and you were wishing that you had it here... and BAM! Now you have it," said Logan.

"I would argue with you, but for the past two weeks I have seen the unexplainable. You will have to teach me more about this later," said Josh.

"Think about it like this, Josh, everything that you have seen during your life had two creation periods. First, it was created in someone's mind, and then it physically manifested on Earth," Logan further explained.

"So, if I thought about my martial arts dojo right now..."

Before Josh could even finish the sentence, he was at the dojo where he studied martial arts. This is where Josh learned how to defend himself and the people that he loved. It was a place of discipline, honor, and respect. It was one of the places that would prepare him to face his challenges in life. The only light in the dojo was from the outside windows. There was no class in session, and they were the only two in the place.

"Yes, if you think about the dojo it will appear," Logan laughed.

"This is crazy... so I get to pick all of the places we go for the rest of my time with you?" Josh asked.

"Not exactly... I just thought it would be fun to let you see how powerful you really are," Logan replied.

As they were talking, the back door opened and the lights inside the room began to come on. A gentleman, small in size but with a powerful presence, walked in with a large gym bag. If you saw him on the street, you would not think that he was a martial arts master. His size didn't matter because he had the heart of a lion and was skilled beyond belief. That was the man that taught Josh what he knew about martial arts, and that knowledge ultimately saved the pregnant woman's life at the bank.

"That is my teacher, Logan. Grand Master Andrew Marshall," Josh said.

"And a great teacher he is," Logan replied.

"I've learned so much more than just martial arts from him. He taught me about life," Josh explained.

The front door of the dojo opened and 17-year-old Josh walked in with his mother Sarah. The teenage Josh had on sweat pants, and a black and orange letterman jacket from his high school. He didn't look happy about being there at all. His mom had her hand on his shoulder as they approached the gentleman at the desk off to the side of the room.

"Welcome to the School of Survival Allegiance. My name is Andrew Marshall, but they call me GM," said the instructor.

"Hello, I'm Sarah Stokes. This is my oldest son Joshua. He wants to take classes here," she said.

"I don't want to take classes here," Josh jumped in right away.

"Well Joshua, we would not want you to do anything that you don't want to do," GM replied.

"Josh, don't be rude," Sarah nudged Josh as she spoke.

"Sir, I'm a wrestler. My dad was a wrestler. I like karate movies, but I don't want to take classes. It's not real fighting, it just looks good. Besides, once somebody has a good hold on you, there isn't much you can do. I'm ranked No. 2 in the state and No. 5 in the nation among wrestlers. This isn't really worth my time. I'd only be interested if it would make me a better wrestler," Josh said.

"Josh is a great athlete, but his father wants him to be more disciplined," Sarah explained.

"Well Josh," said GM "it's good that you don't want to learn karate. We teach Jujitsu here."

"Isn't it all the same?" asked Josh.

"Not at all. Why don't you kick off your shoes and step on the mat with me, please. Since you are taller than me, and you are such a great wrestler, I'm sure you can show me a thing or two."

Logan and Josh watched from afar. Logan could see the excitement in Josh's face as he watched the younger version of himself. Then that look of excitement turned to a look of slight pain. "What's wrong, Josh?" Logan asked.

"He's about to whoop my butt, that's what's wrong. I was a know-it-all, and I quickly realized that I didn't know much as soon as got on that mat."

The younger Josh did everything in his power to take down GM Marshall, but it was to no avail. He was flipped, thrown, taken down, swept, and every other thing imaginable in a matter of two minutes. Every time Josh would try to attack from a different angle, GM would counter him in a way that was too fast for Josh's comprehension. It was as if he knew what Josh was thinking before Josh himself. His mother chuckled as he got tossed around like a rag doll. GM did nothing to hurt him physically, but Josh's pride took a slight beating that day. Eventually, he had had enough and was ready to stop trying. He was out of breath.

"How did you do all of those moves?!" the younger Josh asked with a new found enthusiasm.

"It's what we do here, but you wouldn't be interested in learning remember?" GM replied.

"No, no, I'm interested. I apologize for my attitude earlier sir."

"Apology accepted, Josh. You can't learn anything until you know that you don't know everything. Let's see what days work best for you to get in our classes here."

As they stepped off the mat, Logan and Josh headed to the door. "This is the man that taught me the true art of self defense. That woman in the bank would have died if I hadn't learned something new from him back there. I'm ready to go back to my room..." and before Josh could say "now" he was back in his room. He bid Logan farewell and started to write:

Be open to learn about new things that interest you: Erwin G. Hall once said, "An open mind is the beginning of self-discovery and growth. We can't learn anything new until we can admit that we don't know everything." The cup that is completely full has no more room to be filled with anything else. We have to be willing to accept the fact that we can always learn more. As we grow and expand our thinking we can grow the other areas of our lives.

Josh took the note, folded it, put it in an envelope and left it on the desk, then went to sleep. While he slept, another angel came in the room and took the envelope.

DAY 16

Josh's routine was consistent by now. Breakfast and exercise were usually part of his day. Then he waited for Logan to arrive to see where they would be heading. Josh went to gaze out of his window and he noticed that the scenery looked just like the campus of the university he attended for undergrad. He knew that the lesson of the day was going to come from someone there, but he had no idea who it would be this time. It was easy for him to begin daydreaming as he looked out of the window. The beauty of the campus was accented by all sorts of flowers and greenery. Josh was not paying attention to what was going on behind him as Logan tip-toed toward him and tapped him on the shoulder.

Completely startled, Josh turned around and found himself in the office of his academic advisor, Dr. Brian Brockworth. He was an interesting man. He had a full beard, often smoked a pipe, and would look across the desk at his visitors over the top of his glasses. Dr. Brockworth was co-chair of the Political Science division in which Josh was a star pupil.

"You scared the crap out of me, Logan!"

"Sorry Josh, that wasn't my intent. Who's the guy in the smoker's jacket with the Sherlock Holmes pipe?"

"That's 'Doc Brock,' my advisor and professor. He had a huge influence on me in college."

As they looked on, the younger Josh knocked on the door and stuck his head in to see if Dr. Brockworth was busy.

"Doc, you got a minute?" the younger Josh asked.

"There are one thousand four hundred forty minutes in a day, and I have used approximately half of them being it is around high noon right now. I have roughly seven hundred eighteen left," Dr. Brockworth said as he checked his watch.

Logan looked at Josh and asked, "Does he always talk like that?" but Josh just signaled Logan to keep quiet as he watched the interaction between him and one of his favorite professors. The younger Josh came into the office and took a seat in front of Dr. Brockworth. The room was decorated with books from around the world on a variety of topics.

"Doc, I got my LSAT scores back. I did a lot better than I thought I would do. It should be no problem for me to get into a top tier law school," said Josh.

"Congratulations are in order. You managed to get impeccable grades and pass the LSAT despite being a wild frat boy along with all of your other extracurricular activities."

"Wild?" Josh said as he laughed. "Wild is a relative term, sir. I like to think of myself of well-rounded."

"Yes, yes... most politicians like to think of themselves as honest as well. At any rate, how can I help you with my remaining seven hundred fifteen minutes of this day?" Doc asked.

"Doc, I don't know if I will be a good lawyer," Josh stated with concern.

"Poppycock! You are one of the best students in the program. When you put your mind to a task, you usually get it done unless you are distracted by that Latin tutor of yours I've seen you gallivanting around campus with," Dr. Brockworth said as he looked over the top of his glasses and stuffed more tobacco into his hand-carved pipe from Dubai.

"I know, Doc. I don't doubt my ability to get through law school. I just don't have the passion to be an attorney. I was going to go just because my parents wanted me to go."

"I see, said the blind man," Dr. Brockworth replied.

"Huh? What did the blind man see?" Josh asked.

"It's a figure of speech, Josh. It just means that I understand now. As your friend and your advisor, I would have to tell you not to go to law school if you don't want to be an attorney. If you have another passion in life that you want to go after, then go for it. As long as it doesn't compromise your morals, you will be fine," said Doc.

"Wow, that is not what I expected to hear from you, Doc. I thought you were going to tell me how many people would want to be in my position," Josh said.

"Why would I spend the remainder of my seven hundred eleven minutes of my day telling you what you already know, Mr. Stokes? When I was about your age, my father wanted me to take over the family company. He had been priming me to be his successor for years. As a child, I went on business trips with him. He taught me the daily operations of the business by the time I was 13 years old. The summer before my senior year of high school, I ran the company when my father took ill. His brother ran the company while I was away at college, and when I was getting ready to graduate I had to tell my family that I was going to be a teacher because that is where my heart was. I gave up running Brockworth Billiards Company so that I could be here to help shape the young minds of people like you Josh, and I would do it all over again if I had to."

"Wait a second, Doc! You are telling me that your family is the same family that makes the professional pool tables! Those are Brockworth tables that all the pros on TV play on! WOW!" Josh said with amazement.

"Josh, the most important thing to me was not the money. The most important thing to me was selecting a career that I could be excited about getting up for in the morning. There are millions of ways to make money. I did well in the stock market as a young adult." Dr. Brockworth replied.

"Thanks, Doc Brock! I know what I am going to do now. I may still apply to law school as a backup plan, but I have a better idea of where I'm heading. Enjoy your remaining seven hundred one minutes of your day!"

The younger Josh got up and left the office and Dr. Brockworth took out a book of matches to light his pipe. Logan and Josh looked at each other and Josh nodded his head giving the signal that he was ready to go. In the blink of an eye, he was back in his room and immediately ran to the desk to write:

Find a career or business that you can be passionate about: When you are involved in a career or business that you love, it doesn't really feel like work. Many people hate their jobs. The people that love what they do seem to have a better chance at success. If you can work in an industry that you are passionate about, you will go further and be happier.

Josh took the note, folded it, put it in an envelope and left it on the desk, then went to sleep. While he slept, another angel came in the room and took the envelope.

DAY 17

When Josh woke up on this day, not only was he hungry, he also had a major headache. Logan arrived as Josh forced himself to eat. The pain was a bit much, and he was having a hard time functioning. Logan could see the pain in his face. Josh didn't even notice that Logan had arrived. He was so consumed by the pain that he was almost in tears.

"Josh, I can see you are in pain," Logan said.

"I can barely move. What's wrong with me Logan?" Josh asked.

"Well, you are almost three weeks in. Your body and your spirit are reconnecting. That usually doesn't happen until the end of a journey, but you are so healthy that your recovery is faster than most people's," Logan explained.

"Is there something I can do for the pain?" Josh asked, looking as though he was going to pass out.

"Yes, you can push through the pain. That's what you have done your whole life, Josh. I am not trying to downplay what you are going through, but it is up to you to fight with everything that you have and get through this. What do you want to do?" asked Logan.

"Let's go!" Josh said, as he mustered up the strength to get through the lesson of the day.

Logan instantly transported them to a seminar session at Revolutionary Education, Inc. There were about 150 people in the seminar. Josh and Logan were in the back of the room when Josh realized where he was. At this point in time, he was 24 years old. He had some success in business already, but he was always looking for ways to better himself. He always had the attitude that "those up close get the most," so he was sitting on the second row of the class. The only reason he wasn't on the front row was because all the seats were taken before he got there. About three seats over from him sat a young lady with a serious look on her face. She hid her beauty behind her pinned up hair, and glasses that made her look like a librarian. You could tell that she didn't want to be recognized or talked to. She was there for business.

"Who is the lady you keep glancing at?" Logan asked Josh in the back of the room.

"That's Dagny, my ex-wife... well, we weren't married at the time. This is where we met," Josh explained.

"She isn't paying any attention to you," Logan said.

"Wise guy. I still have a headache. Can you hush for a moment so I can get through this, please?" Josh pleaded.

During the seminar, participants would come to the microphone and share various things. They would talk about life, business, family, challenges, successes, and an array of other topics. The class had no boundaries. It was structured, but it evolved based on the participants there. When the young lady that Josh had his eye on went to the microphone to speak, Josh was captivated. He wasn't as interested in her looks as he was her personality. She was beautiful, but that wasn't what caught his attention. Shortly after she spoke, the Session Leader gave them a dinner break. The younger Josh chased her down in the hallway to introduce himself.

"Excuse me Miss, may I speak with you for a moment?" he asked.

"I'm not interested in whatever you are selling," she replied.

"Selling? Um, I'm not selling anything," he replied.

"Right now, you are selling me a crock of crap. What are your motives, sir?" she asked.

"My name is…" Josh started.

"Joshua Stokes, young entrepreneur, blah, blah, blah. You said that during the seminar. What do you want?" she said with a stoic look on her face.

"We both need to eat, right? I was wondering if you could look over some of the financials and business plans for my company over dinner. You seem to be on top of your game when it comes to business," Josh said.

"I'm not interested in dating you Mr. Stokes!" she uttered, still with the same look on her face.

"I'm not trying to have a date, I'm trying to have a meal," Josh replied.

"How many women have you used that line on?" she asked.

"Honestly… just one," Josh said with a smile.

She finally gave in and agreed to go to dinner with Josh. As they ate, they talked about life and business. Josh wanted to keep his word, and he pulled out his briefcase with the company projections and other paperwork in it. She reviewed the documentation, and with a slightly raised eyebrow she told him, "You are playing too small."

"Excuse me?" he said as if he was slightly insulted.

"You are holding back. There is a lot of room for growth, but you are acting like a coward," she said to Josh with a straight face.

"I don't agree with you," he said in an angry tone.

"The great thing about the truth is that it doesn't care if you agree or not. Instead of risking some of the profit you made two years ago, you saved it all. You didn't come up with any new acquisition plans. You recognized potential market share on Page 4 of this report, but you didn't implement any new strategies to capture it. Need I go on?" she asked.

Josh's feeling were hurt, but he knew she was telling the truth. He quickly signaled for the waitress to bring the check.

"I will pay for my own food, thank you," Dagny stated.

"I'll pay, no problem," Josh responded.

"I don't need your money, sir. I do well enough to afford my own food," she said flatly.

"I'll pay for dinner, and the next time we do dinner it will be for the purpose of me getting to know you better," Josh stated with absolute certainty.

"I'm not interested..." she started as Josh cut her off.

"Yes you are, and you will have dinner with me. Dagny, if you can look me in the eye and tell me that you honestly aren't interested, I'll walk away and we never have to speak again. You said I play too small, well I'm taking your advice now. I don't want to live the rest of my life wondering what would happen if I didn't play full out right now. In life and business, I have to go for the gusto, right?"

The two locked eyes in a stare down for what seemed like an eternity. He won. She agreed to have dinner again. Josh paid for their meals, and they got up to return to the seminar. Logan and spirit-Josh watched them walk out of the restaurant. Josh gave Logan the nod, signaling that he was ready to go.

"You two sure had some energy between you. I'm surprised you didn't stay married," Logan said as he rubbed his head.

"Yep, she's an amazing woman. Our marriage didn't work out, but we are still great friends. We have two beautiful kids and some great memories. We realized that we needed to show our girls what a healthy relationship looks like, and ours just wasn't it. I am happy that she is still a part of my life, and we are adult enough to realize that the most important thing is that we take care of our girls. I learned a lot from her. I need to write down my thoughts before they escape me," Josh said.

Logan left and Josh sat at the desk as he did every other night. The headache had subsided, and he was able to write with a clear conscious and a sound mind:

Play full out: If you are going to participate in something, give it your best! The only thing worse than not trying at all, is trying with little effort. When you give something your best shot, you have done all that you can. When you don't give something your best, there is always the looming "what if I had..." question that you can never get rid of. You may not always get the results that you desire, but you have to learn to take risks and go after what you want with all-out massive action.

Josh took the note, folded it, put it in an envelope and left it on the desk, then went to sleep. While he slept, another angel came in the room and took the envelope.

DAY 18

On the 18th day of this amazing journey, Josh woke up to the voice of Jim Rohn playing on a small CD player sitting on his desk. He was shocked to see it there next to the picture of his daughters, but then he remembered that Logan told him he could think things into existence. His head was hurting when he woke up, so he sat on the side of the bed and focused on making the pain go away. He thought about what he wanted to eat for breakfast, and it appeared in his room as well. He thought about different clothing, and instantly he was dressed in a suit and tie. He thought about Logan, and his door swung open revealing his tour guide, also wearing a suit and tie.

"This thinking magic thing is pretty cool!" Josh exclaimed.

"It is one of the most powerful gifts that God has given to mankind," Logan replied.

I wish I had learned about this sooner!" Josh said with amazement.

"You did," said Logan, and with the snap of a finger, they were at a family holiday party. It was being held at Josh's Aunt Sharon's house. It was the house that Josh's grandparents lived in, and where Josh's mom grew up with her five siblings. Sharon was the youngest of the siblings, and she moved into the house after Josh's grandparents passed away.

"We used to have so much fun with our family," Josh said as he watched several family members dance around and play games.

"Geez, Louise you have a big family!" Logan exclaimed as several kids went running by.

"There I am over there," Josh said as he noticed himself at around 10 years old.

Young Josh was playing a game with his older cousin Kathy. By the look on his face, he wasn't doing too well. Kathy was teasing Josh to the point where he was about to scream. That's when Aunt Sharon pulled Josh to the side to speak with him

"Josh-Mosh, why are you letting Kathy get under your skin like that?" his aunt asked.

"I can't win, and she keeps teasing me!" Josh replied.

"Why don't you think you can beat her?" she asked.

"Because she always wins," he answered.

"Why does she always win?" Sharon asked as she wiped the tears from Josh's face.

"Because she is better than me," he replied.

"I don't think that's the case Josh-Mosh. Your high score in the game is higher than her high score in the game. If you really think about it, you have done better than she has ever done before. It is my belief that the only reason you can't beat her is because you think you can't beat her. I want you to see it in your mind right now. Visualize yourself as the winner. You can do anything you put your mind to. You can do this with a game, your homework, or anything in life. What you think about, you bring about. Now get back over there and show her who's boss!"

Sharon sent Josh back over to play the game with his older cousin. A few minutes later, Josh let out a victory yell that startled everybody in the house! All the family members ran over to see what was happening and why Josh was shouting at the top of his lungs. Not only had he beaten his cousin, he also beat every other high score on the game. He ran over to his aunt, gave her a huge hug, and said, "Thanks auntie! I love you!"

Josh and Logan, dressed like business tycoons, looked at each other and smiled. Logan knew that Josh was ready to get back to the room so that he could write down the lesson for the day.

"Josh-Mosh?" Logan asked with an uncontrollable laugh.

"Hush! Auntie Sharon is the ONLY person who can call me that!" Josh replied.

Upon returning, Josh took off his suit, hung it in the closet that he thought into existence, and sat at the desk and began to write:

What you think about, you bring about: Never underestimate the power of your thoughts. Your mind does not know the difference between fantasy and reality. If you think negative thoughts, negativity will show up in your life. If you think positive thoughts, positive things will show up in your life. Ralph Waldo Emerson said, "A man is what he thinks about all day long." Knowing that, only think about what you want to become reality.

Josh took the note, folded it, put it in an envelope and left it on the desk, then went to sleep. While he slept, another angel came in the room and took the envelope.

DAY 19

Joshua Stokes woke up with pure excitement in his heart this day. Still amazed by this "think magic" he discovered, His room now became a fully furnished house. It was almost identical to his home in the real world, except there were some major upgrades. He had a walk-in closet with plenty of suits, as well as casual clothing. There was an exercise room in the basement of the house that would put other gyms to shame. He also had a personal chef to cook his morning meals. The only thing he was unable to master was the ability to make a door that would take him exactly where he wanted to go. He sat in his home office reading a book as Logan rang the doorbell. Josh's butler opened the door and let Logan in.

"This is a little excessive, isn't it?" Logan asked.

"Excessive is a matter of opinion." Josh replied.

"You didn't have a butler on Earth though," Logan quickly rebutted.

"Only because I hadn't thought about having one," Josh laughed.

"What are you reading?" Logan asked.

"*The Magic of Thinking BIG*, by Dr. David Schwartz," Josh answered.

"That explains the new grandiose living quarters you've created for yourself," said Logan.

"This is actually the first personal development book I was ever given. One of my aunts sent it to me during my senior year of college. I didn't understand the value of it at the time, but I read it anyway. I didn't grasp the concepts in the book until much later in life," Josh explained.

Logan snapped his fingers, and as expected, the scenery changed. They were now in Seattle, Washington at the airport. Josh was still in his pajamas, so he closed his eyes and envisioned himself in a nice suit and tie. He was an impeccable dresser. They were near Gate A7 as the passengers began to exit the jet bridge. A young Joshua Stokes, a few years out of college, stepped through the doorway and looked around.

"Wow, this is the day I met one of my mentors," spirit-Josh whispered to Logan.

"Why are you whispering? Nobody can hear you... let alone see you, 'Mr. Dress-To-Impress' Stokes," Logan said in a joking manner.

"Whatever! You're just mad because I have better fashion sense than you do," Josh laughed.

Logan and well-dressed Josh followed the younger Josh to the baggage claim area. The younger Stokes was met at the bottom of the escalator by a driver holding up a sign with his name on it. Josh had never experienced anything like this before. He was wearing headphones so that he could listen to his favorite artist's latest album. The driver followed him to the baggage carousel, retrieved his bags, and took him to the limo that was waiting outside. Josh had been accepted into a mentoring program where he would be paired up with Marcus Krouse, one of the nation's most influential businessmen in his industry. Mr. Krouse was named "Mr. Healthy, Wealthy, & Wise" several years in a row. He had built several successful organizations and frequently was invited to speak all over the world. Josh was honored to meet him, and extremely excited that he would get to spend two whole weeks with his new mentor.

"Good afternoon Joshua, it's a pleasure to meet you," Mr. Krouse said as Josh entered the limo.

"Thank you, sir. The pleasure is all mine."

"Please, call me Marcus. We have a lot to pack into these two weeks we have together," Krouse said.

"Yes sir… I mean Marcus. I'm sorry. My parents taught me to always respect my elders," Josh explained.

"You have my permission to call me Marcus. You should always call a person what he or she asks you to address them as," Marcus said.

"Yes sir… I mean Marcus. I'll try my best," Josh said with an awkward laugh.

"Henry, can you please turn the audio series back on that I was listening to?" Marcus requested to the driver.

The audio began to play, and Josh was surprised that there was no music. There were only the words of the gentleman speaking on philosophies and principles that Josh was unfamiliar with. Marcus pulled out his notepad, and began to take notes on what the speaker was lecturing on. Josh put his headphones back on and began to nod his head to the tunes that only he could hear. Marcus noticed that Josh wasn't paying attention to the lecture, and he asked Josh to take his headphones off for a moment.

"What are you listening to, if you don't mind me asking?" Marcus inquired.

"Just a few tunes from some of my favorite bands. I can give it to the driver if you want to listen in too," Josh said, hoping Marcus would agree.

"What did you feed your brain for breakfast this morning?" Marcus asked.

"I don't understand sir... I mean Marcus," Josh said sounding confused.

"What did you read or listen to that is feeding your brain or mind with positive programming?" asked Marcus.

"I'm not exactly sure how to answer that," Josh said with a puzzled look on his face.

As this conversation was taking place, the limousine pulled into the driveway of a beautiful estate. The lawn was well manicured, and there was a beautiful waterfall near the entrance of the home. Elegant marble stairs led to gigantic French doors. The driver retrieved the luggage from the trunk as Marcus escorted Josh into his home. Josh was amazed not only at the size of the home, but the opulence of it as well. The first place that Marcus took Josh was to the library of the house.

"If you are wondering how I became successful, this is part of the equation," Marcus told Josh as they walked into the library.

"Wow, have you read all of these books?" Josh asked.

"Yes. If you look to the east, you will see the audio collection as well," Marcus pointed out.

"Oh, like the boring guy you were listening to in the car?" asked Josh.

"That boring guy makes about $18.7 million a month," Marcus laughed.

"You've got to be kidding me!" Josh exclaimed.

"The best way to truncate your potential for success is to be closed-minded to those who have more knowledge and experience than you," Marcus added.

"Truncate?" Josh asked.

"There's a dictionary on the table over there. If ever I use a word that you don't understand, look it up. You will remember it better if you read the answer as opposed to me just giving it to you. Listen, I'm not saying that you should never listen to music. I have my favorite artists that I listen to as well. The thing that I realize is that those artists will not pay my bills for me. I make sure my mental diet is filled with things that will add to my life. Things that will get my mind headed in the right direction. I read books that teach me what others did to become successful. This library you are standing in is worth more than the cost of the books and audios that are in it. These shelves are lined with the treasure maps that will get you where you want to go in life. It's open to you 24 hours a day. All I ask is that you put things back exactly where you found them when you are done." Marcus stated as he was leaving the room.

Young Josh stood there in amazement. He had never seen so many books in a person's home. His father had a den with a bookcase in it, but this was a room filled with books on almost everything that a businessman would want to read. He walked over to one of the tables, and to his surprise he saw an autographed copy of "The Magic of Thinking BIG." He sat down and began to thumb through the pages with a greater curiosity than when he read the copy his aunt sent him in college.

Josh and Logan watched as the young Josh pulled several books off of the library shelves. After several minutes went by, Josh signaled to Logan that he was ready to go. Logan snapped his fingers, and instantly they were back in the small room Josh was originally given. Josh smiled at Logan and bid him farewell. As soon as Logan was gone, Josh snapped his fingers and the room changed back into the home he had created for himself earlier that day. He went to the library of the house and sat at the desk where he began to write:

Be aware of your mental diet: Just like the food you eat has an impact on your health and body weight, the things that you put into your mind have an impact on your mental health and well-being. Your "brain food" actually can impact your physical life too. That is why it is important to feed your mind with ideas that will have the type of impact that you really desire. Reading positive books, attending stimulating seminars, and listening to audio series that promote the growth and development of your thinking will ultimately have you in tip-top mental shape. Physically and mentally, you are what you eat.

Josh took the note, folded it, put it in an envelope and left it on the desk, then went to sleep. While he slept, another angel came in the room and took the envelope.

DAY 20

When Logan arrived at the intergalactic-Stokes-residence, Josh was just wrapping up breakfast while trading stocks on his laptop computer. He had the morning paper next to him as well. There were fresh cut flowers on the table, and a cup of green tea rested in front of a chair where Josh suggested Logan should sit. Logan was a bit surprised that Josh conjured up a newspaper and laptop. After all, this was not really his life on Earth.

"Josh… a newspaper? Aren't you getting a little too crazy with this whole thought process thing?" Logan asked.

"If indeed I do return to a normal life, I don't want to skip a beat. It's bad enough I've spent all this time away from my family, businesses, and investments. I have to be able to recoup my losses when this is over," Josh replied.

"What if you don't get through this alive, Josh?" Logan asked.

"Then I will die knowing that I did everything in my power to make a difference in the lives of others," Josh said as he looked up from his laptop at Logan.

Josh was getting up from the table just as Logan transported them to Addler Middle School. This is where Tiffany attended 4th grade. They were in the principal's office as Josh and Dagny were escorted in by the school secretary. Tiffany was already sitting in the office with her chin down so that she wouldn't have to look at her parents as they walked in. Josh sat right next to his daughter and put his finger under her chin. "Head up, Scooch. No kid of mine is allowed to walk around with their head down."

The principal began to explain to Josh and Dagny that Tiffany had been caught with her mom's lipstick, fingernail polish, eye shadow, and mascara. Tiffany would come to school and charge the other little girls to do their makeup. When confronted about it, she told her teacher that she didn't have any makeup, and she didn't know why the other little girls would make up a story like that about her. The teacher actually found the makeup in Tiffany's backpack. She was caught red handed. Josh and Dagny got to the school around the time that the children were to be let out, so they took their daughter home in the car with them. Spirit-Josh and Logan sat in the back seat with Tiffany.

"Young lady, what do you have to say for yourself?" Dagny asked.

"Well at least she was starting a business," Josh laughed

"This is not a laughing matter Joshua!" Dagny said in a stern voice.

"But mom, I was just trying to make money to help you and dad," Tiffany blurted out.

"Help me and your mom?" Josh asked.

"Yes, I heard you talking to Uncle Greg about how you lost a lot of money on a bad investment, and that we may have to sell the house!" Tiffany began to cry.

Dagny and Josh looked at each other. Their hearts dropped when they understood why Tiffany did what she did. She was a good kid, and she only wanted to help. This was the first time that she had ever gotten into trouble. Dagny wasn't happy about it, but she knew that Tiffany was ashamed of telling a lie to her teacher. She wanted to assure her that everything was going to be OK.

"Baby, Mommy and Daddy will be just fine. We are working through this rough patch in Daddy's business. I may go back to work soon to help out as well. You didn't have to lie about having the makeup, though. It is never good to tell a lie," Dagny explained.

"You mean like when Nana calls, and you tell me to tell her you're not home so you don't have to talk to her?" Tiffany asked.

"You don't like talking to my mother!?" Josh asked.

"Or Daddy, like when you tell me that smoking is bad for you, but then you and Uncle Greg go on the back deck and smoke those Cuban cigars that you told Mommy you threw away?" Tiffany went on.

"Josh! I knew I smelled cigar on you! You know Cuban cigars are illegal in the U.S.," said Dagny.

"Or when the both of you..." Tiffany started.

"Enough!" Dagny and Josh interrupted her in unison.

"Gosh, I was just asking questions," Tiffany replied.

"Baby, we are sorry. Your mother and I should have set better examples for you," Josh said.

"Yes dear, your Dad and I are sorry. How about this... let's all make a promise to tell the truth and do the right thing all the time. We can pinkie swear right now," Dagny suggested.

All three agreed on the idea, and they entwined their pinkies together smiling. They made a deal, and the Stokes family always kept their word. Even when the task that they promised to do was difficult, they followed through with it. Josh signaled to Logan that he was ready to head back so that he could write the lesson of the day on paper. Logan transported them back to Josh's well-thought-out temporary home, and Josh immediately went to his desk to write:

Set good examples for your children or the children around you: Kids are very impressionable. They often mimic adults. If you speak and act differently than you would want your kids to act (or the kids that you happen to be around, if you don't have any of your own), then you may want to change your actions. "Do as I say, not as I do" doesn't really work with children. What you do always speaks louder than what you say. Watch your actions... because the children you influence are watching your actions too.

Josh took the note, folded it, put it in an envelope and left it on the desk, then went to sleep. While he slept, another angel came in the room and took the envelope.

DAY 21

When Logan came to meet Josh on this day, he found him deep in paperwork. Josh was acting as if he was in the real world. It was a far more complicated scene than him at the table with a newspaper and his laptop. This time, he had stacks of reports near him, charts and graphs pinned up around his home office, books sprawled out all over his desk, and a pencil in his mouth that he had been gnawing on all morning. He didn't even notice that Logan was there to start the voyage of the day.

"Excuse me your highness, your chariot awaits you," Logan greeted Josh.

"Give me a few minutes please. I've got to figure this out," Josh said without even lifting his head.

"Josh, you take yourself way too seriously at times. None of this matters right now," Logan explained.

"Hey, I have to stay on top of my game," Josh replied.

"Josh-Mosh, I'm trying to be nice. Remember I'm the expert here," Logan said.

"I told you that my aunt is the only one allowed to call me that!" Josh exclaimed as he stood up and walked toward Logan.

Logan snapped his fingers, but nothing appeared to really change. They were in Josh's home office. Everything looked almost exactly the same. Josh was still walking toward Logan when he heard the telephone ring. He turned around to go back to his desk, but to his surprise he was already sitting there. Logan had transported them to the weekend before the incident at the bank. Josh stood there in awe, looking at himself at his desk. He was on the phone with one of his attorneys he had access to through

LegalShield. He was working feverishly trying to figure out some legal issues that were keeping him from making an international business deal. That's when his youngest daughter Miranda walked in.

"Daddy, when are we going to go outside and play?" she asked.

"I'm on the phone Pooka, give Daddy an hour to finish up," he whispered to her.

"But you said that three hours and twenty-two minutes ago," she said in a disappointed voice.

"If Daddy doesn't get his work done, we won't be able to go to Hawaii in June," he sighed.

"Dad, I don't care if we go to Hawaii or not. You will be on your phone and your computer all day there too! You need to take some time to smell the roses!" she whined as she began to cry.

"How old are you again?!" Josh laughed.

"It's not funny. My Daddy-Daughter time is severely limited due to your business shenanigans!" she said.

"No seriously, how old are you?!" he asked.

"I'm 5 years old, but my mind is at least 9 or 10. Possibly 11," she replied.

Josh ended the call with his attorney, got up from his desk, picked up his daughter into his arms, and walked out of his office. The spirit-Josh stood there watching them exit with tears in his eyes. He knew exactly where they were going. He remembered it like it was yesterday. That day, he put everything on hold and took his girls out for "Daddy-Daughter Day" around the city. They had a blast that day. He even let them eat massive amounts of junk food as a treat. It didn't happen often, but that day, they ate like pigs. They visited several museums, parks, and even took a bike ride around Lake Michigan. Logan snapped his fingers and things were back to as they were before the lesson of the day took place. Still with tears in his eyes, he bid Logan farewell and began to write:

Enjoy the beauty around you: There are some natural wonders that we don't take advantage of. The beauty of the world is at our fingertips! Take time to watch the sun set one evening. Take a walk through the park and smell the flowers. Visit a museum and learn something new. Whatever you have around you, take the time to enjoy it. Enjoy the people you have around you as well. If you do this, you will develop a greater appreciation of life.

Josh took the note, folded it, put it in an envelope and left it on the desk, then went to sleep. While he slept, another angel came in the room and took the envelope.

~~

So you've made it through 75 percent of the story. Yes, I'm talking to you again. You should be used to this by now. Are you enjoying this so far? Josh has some adorable kids doesn't he? But the story is not done yet. Congratulations on getting this far, but 75 percent is only a "C" on the grading scale. You don't strike me as a "just average" type of person. I am sure you will see this all the way through. By the way, you really need to enroll in LegalShield, just like Josh did. It's a real service that gives you access to attorneys for various things for less than a cup of coffee a day. When is the last time you had your Last Will and Testament updated? Have you ever wanted to just ask a question, or get a contract reviewed before you signed it? Check out this website for more information, and you can even enroll there if you like what you see.

www.theplanforyou.com

Again, congrats on getting this far! It's time for what may be the final week of Josh's life. Are you as anxious as I am to see what happens next? Well, I guess we need to go find out. I'll join you... let's see what happens in week No. 4.

BOOK 4

I am so happy to see you here, figuratively speaking. Obviously, I can't "see" you from the pages of a book, but I know you are here. It's crazy how easy it is to get caught up in a story. You have come this far, and it would be a shame to stop now. You would have to go the rest of your life wondering if Josh makes it out. We both know that you don't want to live with that. Let's see what Joshua and Logan are up to. Can you believe it's Day 22 already?! OK, OK, I'll stop rambling now. It's time to jump back into the story.

DAY 22

The third week of Josh's journey is over. It really doesn't seem like it has been that long, does it? Funny how time flies when you're having fun. Logan arrived at Josh's temporary home... you do remember that this is temporary, right? Anyway, Logan arrived and Josh was anxiously waiting. He had on a three-piece suit that looked like the finest designer in Italy made it for him. His shoes appeared to be hand-crafted. The color combination of his shirt and tie matched so well, he looked as though he could model for a men's fashion magazine.

"Why so spiffy, Josh?" Logan asked.

"I feel better when I look better. It's a psychological thing," he answered.

"Well, you may want to change clothes. Something a bit more athletic would work better today," Logan said.

That's when Josh noticed that Logan had on shorts, which were a little too short in Josh's opinion, a tank top, and a head band. Logan's socks were pulled up to his knees. The fact that he had wings made the whole thing look even crazier. Logan looked like an NBA basketball player from the mid 1970s.

"I guess you don't pay attention to fashion trends?" Josh laughed.

"I'm giving you 3 seconds to change clothes!" Logan replied as if he was offended.

Josh thought himself into some athletic apparel just as Logan snapped his fingers. The scenery changed to a college outdoor stadium. It had to be at least 95 degrees outside, and the sun was hot and bright, and the stands were filled to capacity. This was the state finals for track and field. Leonidis Catholic High School was close to having several winners in different events. A younger Josh, a 16-year-old high school junior, was sitting on a bench next to his friend Trevor Cook. Trevor was one of the best shot put throwers in the school's history, but he wasn't doing so well this day. There were several other team members gathered in the area as well.

"TC, what's going on man?" Josh asked.

"The guy from St. Franklin is kicking my butt. Every throw of his has been better than mine. It will be impossible for me to win this event," Cook commented.

"Yeah, and the guys from East St. Lewis are as fast as rockets! Did you see their uniforms? They look like Spider Man with those total body spandex things on!" teammate Noah Crandal added.

"We did good enough to get here, but it's impossible to beat all these other teams. They are the best in the state!" Mike Fletcher chimed in.

Mr. Eddie Anders, the head track coach, walked into the circle to talk to his athletes. He was a short and stocky man with a booming voice. He was fun to be around, but he took his job very seriously. The team had a massive amount of respect for him because he turned the track and field program around in just a year and a half. The student athletes continued to grumble about how it was impossible for any of them to do well at the state finals. Coach Anders was quiet for about 30 seconds, and then he erupted:

"ENOUGH!" he yelled.

"But coach…" Cook tried to interject.

"BUT NOTHING! I will not have this defeated attitude smother the hard work we put in all year!" Coach belted out.

"How do we beat the best in the state?" Josh queried. "Every other school has more students than us, so they have better athletes to choose from."

"Stokes, of all the people on the team, I never thought I would hear something like that from you. Listen guys, there is NOTHING impossible in the world! NOTHING! Records were made to be beaten, and champions can fall. Who cares if these guys have won state more than us?! Who cares if they have more students than us?! The only thing we care about is kicking their butts until they are black and orange! Years ago, people thought it was impossible to run a 4-minute mile. Now, we have people on this very team who have done it. People thought it was impossible for man to fly. Some of you seniors have been on planes to take college visits because it was possible for the Wright Brothers to make planes that worked. People always want to talk about what's impossible. Well, if you look at how the word is spelled, impossible really means I-M POSSIBLE! Nothing is impossible. Not even a few guys from a small Catholic school on the south side of Chicago taking home the state championship in track and field!"

The entire team was fired up! Every athlete was focused on doing the I-M-possible. The looks on their faces were so serious that people in the stands thought that they were mad. The guys walked toward each event with an unparalleled confidence. They were hungry for victory, and they knew that nothing was impossible. At the end of the day, Leonidis Catholic High School would take home the state championship in track and field.

Logan was highly impressed. He witnessed event after event of total domination by young Josh and his teammates. "You guys kicked some major butt!" he told Josh. As the team headed for the bus, trophy and medals in hand, Josh was happy about going back to this day in his life. It was the day that he learned nothing was too big for him to conquer. When they got back to Josh's temporary home, Logan asked him if he minded sharing what he was going to write. Josh simply said "I'm going to write down the quote from Muhammad Ali that Coach Anders made us memorize. A huge poster hung in the weight room that read:

"Impossible is just a big word thrown around by small men who find it easier to live in the world they've been given than to explore the power they have to change it. Impossible is not a fact. It's an opinion. Impossible is not a declaration. It's a dare. Impossible is potential. Impossible is temporary. Impossible is nothing." –Muhammad Ali-

Josh took the note, folded it, put it in an envelope and left it on the desk, then went to sleep. While he slept, another angel came in the room and took the envelope.

DAY 23

When Logan arrived to take Josh out for the day, he found him laughing hysterically. Josh was watching a video from a real estate and investing guru named James Smith. There were tears in Josh's eyes from laughter. Logan hadn't seen him laugh this much since they met.

"Let's go Josh, we have work to do. The early bird gets the worm," Logan said.

"I don't do worms, but I'll eat your bird!" Josh said as he fell off of the couch laughing.

"Aren't you a vegetarian?" Logan asked in complete confusion.

"I am, but that's what James Smith just said before you got here," Josh said as he continued laughing. "You really need to see this seminar series. He was talking about this one guy who was racist. He told him 'I hope you catch cataracts and your prostate explodes!' for judging some of God's children based on color," Josh went on, still laughing uncontrollably.

"That's not a very nice thing for him to say, but it was kinda funny," Logan snickered.

"As soon as I catch my breath, we can leave," Josh said, still laughing. "This guy is a riot! He also provides some very good investment information."

Logan took Josh back to the home of his parents. It was the summer after his junior year of college. This was the first summer that Josh opted not to get a summer job. He developed some pretty bad habits, one of which was watching television. He became addicted to a couple of "Reality TV" shows, whatever ball games came on, and even watched talk shows. He made time for sitcoms as well. His mother was not pleased with how he was spending his summer. Sarah and Abraham tried to instill good habits in their kids as best as they could. One day, she came home from the bakery she owned and found Josh on the couch stuffing his mouth with pizza and watching television. The whole living room was a mess.

"Joshua Daniel Stokes!" Sarah said as she stood right in front of the television.

"I must be in serious trouble. You used my whole name," Josh answered her.

"Young man, it makes no sense on God's green Earth for you to spend your day in front of the boob tube," she said.

"The what?" he asked.

The boob tube. Idiot box. Television. Or the 'electronic income reducer' as your father calls it," Sarah explained.

"But mom, you act like I do this all the time," Josh whimpered.

"You have been doing this all summer. I just don't want you to develop a bad habit that you will regret later," said Sarah.

"I happen to like Reality TV, mom," Josh argued.

"Why watch Reality TV when you can create your own reality every day? I am not saying that you should never watch TV. There are a couple of shows that I happen to enjoy. What I am saying is that if you spend all of your time watching other people live their dreams of acting, playing sports, or making fools of themselves on trashy talk shows, you end up wasting valuable time that could be used on you living into your purpose. There are people who watch the game, and there are people who make the game happen," said Sarah.

"So you are saying, 'Why sit in the stands when I can be on the field?'" Josh asked.

"Being on the field is OK for a while. But why settle for being on the field when you have the ability to own the team? The only place that success comes before work is in the dictionary. You can't sit on the couch for the rest of the summer, or the rest of your life, and expect to make an impact on the world," Sarah said as she grabbed the remote control to turn off the TV.

Josh and Logan went back to Josh's place so that Josh could write down the lesson for the day. He went to his desk and began to write:

Be a player, not a spectator: In the game of life, there are players and there are spectators. Just like in professional sports, the players get paid large amounts of money while the spectators sit and watch. The players make things happen, and the spectators sit and watch. The players enjoy the thrill of victory, and the spectators sit and watch. If you want things to move in a positive direction in your life, you have to be a player. Don't just sit and watch your life go by hoping for something to happen. Get on the field and make it happen. You don't have to stop there though. You can be an owner and make it happen for others. The most important thing is that you don't settle on just being a spectator.

Josh took the note, folded it, put it in an envelope and left it on the desk, then went to sleep. While he slept, another angel came in the room and took the envelope.

DAY 24

Josh woke up this morning long before Logan arrived. He ate, exercised, and walked around the house looking at old pictures. True, they were pictures he thought up, but something about them seemed different than the ones he remembered in real life. In one particular hallway, there were several pictures of Miranda and Tiffany. Most of the pictures on this wall he had never seen before. The thing that stood out the most to him was the fact that the girls didn't look happy in any of the pictures. As a matter of fact, they were crying in some of them. Logan arrived as Josh was pulling a picture frame off of the wall.

"You've created a nice home in your mind, but now we must travel through time. Hey, I'm a poet and I didn't even know it," Logan laughed.

"Yeah, yeah... that's nice." Josh spoke, but he didn't look away from the picture.

"What's wrong my friend?" asked Logan.

"I created my surroundings, but these pictures of my daughters are not familiar at all," he explained.

"Ah, it's happening. I'm surprised it took this long," Logan replied.

"I don't get it?" said Josh with a puzzled look on his face.

"Where do I start? Um... OK... At some point in the voyage, after a person learns to change their environment through thought, their surroundings are often influenced by the lessons they have learned or will learn. It happens from time to time," Logan explained.

"So what does that have to do with these pictures of my girls?"

Logan instantly transported them to a home that Joshua and Dagny shared around the time that Tiffany was 10 years old and Miranda was just born. Joshua sat at the dining room table as Dagny paced back and forth rapidly. They were in the middle of an argument. When two passionate people disagree, it's not a pretty sight. There were documents scattered all over the place. Both of them had wrinkled foreheads from frowning.

"You make me sick Josh! I don't have to agree with every decision that you make!" Dagny said with a very stern voice.

"I don't care if you agree. This has nothing to do with you," Josh angrily replied.

"What do you mean it has nothing to do with me?! I am your wife!" she said as she tried to refrain from yelling because the kids were upstairs.

"Yes, control freak! You are my wife. Wife does not equate to being my master. Slavery was abolished by the way, just in case you weren't paying attention in history class," Josh said in an extremely smart-aleck tone.

"You know what... I can't take this anymore! I hope that you fail horribly and fall flat on your face. And when you do, me and the girls will not be around to pick you up. I'm done Josh... I'm DONE! I hate you and the girls hate you too!" she yelled.

"FINE! FINE! I wish that God would erase the day I met you! My life would be better if I'd never met you and if you never got pregnant!" Josh yelled back at her.

Just then, Tiffany walked into the room holding her newborn sister. The words of her parents were so sharp, it was as if they cut right through her. She stood there in disbelief looking at both of her parents as tears began to well up in her eyes. She held her baby sister even tighter, and then she turned around and ran out of the room. Josh and Dagny looked at each other with blank stares on both of their faces. After an odd moment of awkward silence, they both left the room to go speak with their daughter.

"Wow, you two were something else!" Logan stated.

"Can we go now, please?" Josh requested.

"What was the argument about anyway?" Logan asked.

"I decided to sell one of the companies I owned before it went under," Josh explained.

"Why was she so mad about that?" Logan asked.

"It was a company that was founded on our wedding anniversary. It was going under big time, but she thought... WHY AM I EXPLAINING THIS TO YOU? Can we go please?" Josh requested again with an irritated tone.

Logan transported them back to Josh's place. Josh sat at his desk looking at the picture of his girls he had pulled off the wall. With tears in his eyes he wrote:

Think before you speak: Pound for pound, the tongue is the strongest muscle in the human body. It has more than just physical strength though. What you speak has power! Words can build, but they can also destroy. They can promote, or they can oppress. They can speak life, or they can invite death. Do not underestimate the power of your words. What you speak has an amazing effect on your life and the lives of those around you. Once you spit them out, you cannot take them back. Make sure you are speaking words that will enhance your life, and the lives of those around you.

Josh took the note, folded it, put it in an envelope and left it on the desk, then went to sleep. While he slept, another angel came in the room and took the envelope.

DAY 25

When Logan arrived to pick up Josh this day, he found him in the exercise facility working out like a mad man. The look on his face was one of absolute focus. To the outsider, it looked as though Josh was training for the Olympics or something. His form while doing every exercise was flawless. Logan was impressed.

"Do you always look so serious when you work out?" Logan asked.

"This is a serious matter," Josh responded, sounding slightly short of breath.

"I hate to burst your bubble Josh. I know this is the fourth week of your journey, but you do realize that you are not actually working your physical body, right?" Logan asked.

"I've heard of the 'angel of death' before, but you are the 'angel of bubble bursting," Josh replied.

Logan continued, "Why are you so obsessed with working out? What made you this way? Can we go to that event in your life?"

"I thought that I only got to select one day or event in my life to go to during this agreement," Josh said.

"You do. You didn't ask to go to that day; I asked you if we could go there," Logan replied.

Josh agreed to take Logan back to his freshman year in high school. They arrived in Josh's old neighborhood. There they found 13-year-old Joshua Stokes walking from the bus stop to his house. Abraham was on vacation, so he had been home all day. Sarah was out bowling with a group of friends, so Josh didn't expect her to be home. Josh was about to put his key in the door when he recognized that it was already open. At first he thought that

Donavan may have left the door open, but then he realized that his younger brother was in an accelerated math program that met after school. Instantly, Josh was concerned about walking into an open house.

"Hello?" he said cautiously as he walked through the door.

"Is anybody home?" He walked around expecting a burglar to jump out at any time. When he walked by the bathroom, he saw the legs of his father lying in the doorway.

"DAD! DAD! What's wrong?!" Josh yelled as he dropped to his knees to see about his father.

Abraham was blue in the face. He was not responding to Josh at all. There was an open bottle of aspirin that had spilled all over the floor. Josh immediately got up and ran for the phone. He dialed 911 with a shaky hand and spoke with a terrified voice.

"Hello 911! I need help! My dad isn't breathing!" he explained.

Within a matter of minutes, an ambulance and paramedics were at the door. They put Abraham on a stretcher and carried him out. Josh was right behind them. He had already called up to the bowling alley to tell his mom what was going on. She picked up Donavan, and they met Josh at the hospital emergency room. The doctor came to the waiting room to address the family.

"I have some good news and some bad news," said the doctor.

"What's the bad news?" Sarah asked.

"Your husband has had a heart attack and needs emergency bypass surgery."

"But he will be OK, right?" Donavan asked.

"That's the good news. They are working on him now. If he makes it through surgery, he should be OK. But he will have to change his eating and exercise habits," the doctor said.

"STOP!" spirit-Josh yelled.

"What's wrong?" Logan asked.

"This is the day that I almost lost my dad. He always has been, and still is my hero. I know that he won't be around forever. I can only imagine how he feels with me being in the hospital... Actually, where are my parents? Wait... I haven't seen them in the hospital at all since the accident," Josh reflected.

Logan broke the news to Josh: "Your dad had another heart attack, Josh. He is in the same hospital, and he is on life support as well. The idea of losing you was too much for him. He didn't know how to take it, and his heart started to fail. He is still alive, for now. Your mother didn't want to see you in the condition that you were in when you first arrived. She has been to see you since the surgery though. She is having a hard time dealing with the possibility of losing two of the most important men in her life."

"This is exactly why I am an exercise fanatic. I need my body to be able to take the stresses of life! The first time my dad had a heart attack, I vowed that I would do everything that I can to stay healthy. I did not want to wait until it was too late. Now you tell me that he is in the hospital again... I can't take much more of this Logan!" Josh said.

"Your journey is almost done, Josh. I think it's best that we go back now," Logan said in a subdued tone.

Logan transported Josh back to his living quarters. Josh couldn't write right away. He was too busy thinking about his father. He wanted to know if he was going to be OK. He wanted to tell his mother not to worry, and that everything was going to be just fine. He wasn't sure that things would turn out well for either of them, though. Yet, Josh found the strength to get to his desk and write the lesson of the day:

Run for your life: That saying typically is used to warn people of danger. Well, running for your life can be a good thing. Running, and most other exercise for that matter, is good for your heart and health. The majority of people in the world have no type of exercise routine. Rest, diet, and exercise are essential for a healthy lifestyle. People who exercise to stay in shape feel better, have more energy, and seem to be able to get more done than those who don't. Exercise can help add years to your life if done consistently and coupled with good eating habits.

Josh took the note, folded it, put it in an envelope and left it on the desk, then went to sleep. While he slept, another angel came in the room and took the envelope.

DAY 26

When Logan arrived on Day 26, Josh was sitting in complete darkness. He had not eaten. He was not interested in exercise. He was not dressed for the voyage of the day. He just sat on the couch staring blankly at the wall. The only thing he could think about was his father.

"Wakey wakey, eggs and bakey!" Logan sang as he opened the curtains to let some light in.

"None of this matters. The light isn't real, nor is this house, the food, the anything," Josh mumbled.

"What is wrong with you, man? You have some so far and now all of a sudden give up? What happened to the lesson Nicole taught you? You don't fail unless you quit!" Logan argued.

"The reality of it all is that I am still in a coma. My dad is in bad shape. The only thing that is certain is that there is uncertainty," Josh said.

"That is nothing new, Mr. Stokes. Life would not be challenging at all if every single moment was predictable. You have lived with the same uncertainty every day, and you made the best of it! Don't change that now!" Logan pleaded.

"I could take calculated risks on Earth though. This is just a waste of time," complained Josh.

"I guess you had something better to do while in a coma," Logan replied.

"That's easy for you to say. You don't understand..." Josh started.

"What I do understand is that you have had some amazing experiences over the past couple of weeks. I can't tell you how the story is going to end, but I do know that you are the author of this book, Joshua Stokes!" Logan said.

Logan snapped his fingers, and instantly they were in a modest apartment with very little furniture. It was Josh's first home after college. A younger version of Josh, around 21 years old, was in the bathroom mirror shaving his face. He had clothes laid out on the bed, and a leather briefcase sitting on the floor next to his nightstand. It was obvious that he was nervous. He tried to keep his hand steady while shaving so that he wouldn't cut himself.

"What are you doing? Didn't I just tell you this was a waste of time?" spirit-Joshua complained.

"I don't know about you, but I have a job to do. That job is to show you what you need to see during the time allotted to us," Logan replied.

The doorbell rang, and the young Josh threw his clothes on and headed out the door. He got in the car with his field trainer Wallace Smith. Josh had taken a position with an employee benefits company, and Wallace had years of experience. At first glance, you wouldn't think he was a millionaire. He was very down to earth, and spoke with a Midwestern accent. Josh requested additional training because he just couldn't seem to get any real traction in the field. Josh hated being below average in anything that he did, but sales was totally new to him.

"Good morning Mr. Smith," Josh said as he got into the car.

"You're a good kid, you can call me Uncle Wally," he stated.

"Um… okay. If you say so," Josh replied.

"I insist. So are you ready to have a HUGE day? We have several enrollments lined up. My wife Caroline said I better come home with a huge stack of apps, so I set a goal to get 93 people to sign up out of every 100 people I present to!" Wallace said.

"That's a lot of apps. I just go in and get what I can get. I'm happy to walk out with whatever I get," Josh reasoned.

"Have you ever fired a hunting rifle before Josh?" Wally asked.

"I'm from Chicago, sir. Not much hunting in the city."

"Well, have you ever fired any type of gun? And if so, what did you shoot at?" Wallace laughed.

"Yes, I have family in law enforcement and I have fired handguns before. We shot at targets," Josh said.

"AH HA! You had something you were aiming for. If you didn't have a target, you would have nothing to shoot for," Wallace said.

"What does that have to do with enrolling people in employee benefits?" asked Josh.

"Your target is your goal! The problem is that you don't set goals. The only difference between the big shot and the little shot is that the big shot kept shooting... and he was shooting at a specific goal. He knows what he is shooting at!" Wallace explained.

"Ahhhh, I see Mr. Smith... I mean Uncle Wally. If I have a goal in mind, I am more likely to hit it!" Josh said as the light bulb in his mind went off.

"Not only do you need a target... YOU NEED A HUGE TARGET! Set some HUGE goals, Josh. You may not always hit them, but at least you will be closer to something big instead of setting a small goal that doesn't push you to do better or be better. Set goals so big that people will laugh at you when they hear them. Before I worked here, I was a grocery store clerk. Who would have ever thought that a man who bagged groceries for a living would one day be a millionaire? It's all because I learned how to set and achieve huge goals. If a good old country boy can do it, I'm sure a city slicker like you will have no problem being successful at anything you set your mind to. Just make sure that goal-setting is a part of your plan for success!" Wallace exclaimed.

Wallace and Josh pulled up to their first appointment. While Wallace was driving, Josh wrote a goal to sign up 100 percent of the people they talked to. They went into the company and made presentations to the staff. The spirit-like Josh motioned to Logan that he was ready to go, and instantly they were back in Josh's home.

"So what happened that day Josh?" Logan asked.

"I didn't hit my goal. I only signed up 96 percent of the people I talked to that day. But it was the biggest commission check I had received since starting the job, " Josh explained.

"I guess Uncle Wally was right after all," Logan said as he left Josh to his usual routine.

Josh sat at his desk, and he noticed a picture of him, Uncle Wally, and Aunt Caroline on his desk. He smiled and began to write:

Set some HUGE goals: Most people never achieve anything in life because they never set goals; or the goals that they do set are too small. You have the power to accomplish world-changing things! Yet 95% of the world chooses to be average. Once you set a HUGE goal, your mind and spirit will come up with ways to achieve it as long as you stay focused on your goal. The Wright Brothers, Thomas Edison, and Alexander Miles are examples of inventors who set HUGE goals and made them happen! The same can happen for you in any field of human endeavor you want to participate in. Set some HUGE goals, work toward them, and success will be yours!

Josh took the note, folded it, put it in an envelope and left it on the desk, then went to sleep. While he slept, another angel came in the room and took the envelope.

DAY 27

This was the 27th day of Josh's journey. He had experienced something that many people couldn't even imagine. For about a month, he and Logan traveled through time visiting moments in his life that helped shape his character. He was reminded of all the people who had contributed to his way of thinking. He even went back to painful times in his life and learned from his mistakes. All of this happened because he was willing to take a chance. He took action when Logan presented him with an opportunity. It was something unfamiliar to him, but he explored it anyway.

When Josh woke up on this day, he was not in the house he thought of in his mind. He was back in the plain room with four white walls and a desk. There was no window and no food. The room looked like it did the first time he saw in. He didn't have the ability to change his clothes anymore either. He jumped out of bed and went to open the door, but it wouldn't budge. He began to panic. He had never experienced claustrophobia until now. That's when Logan appeared behind him.

"Josh, calm down," Logan said as he touched Josh's shoulder.

"Get away from me!" Josh yelled. "What's going on?!" He demanded an answer.

"Josh, your time is almost up," Logan explained.

"I thought we were friends, Logan! What is happening here?!" he yelled.

"Josh, this is what happens toward the end. I'm sorry," said Logan.

"Sorry for what?! So you are the angel of death?" Josh asked as he raised his fists to defend himself against Logan.

"I'm not here to fight you. I am your friend. And we must go," Logan said as he snapped his fingers.

Instantly, they were back at the bank on the day of the robbery. There was complete chaos all around. The spirit-Josh had a heightened sense of awareness. It was as if he was seeing the event through the eyes of every person there. The amount of fear in the room was like nothing he had ever experienced. His heart raced and he began to sweat profusely. Things happened just as he remembered, but this time it was faster. It was more intense. It was like watching an action scene in a movie.

The events occurred in the exact same order. The robbers came in, the pregnant woman started crying, one of the robbers approached her, Josh defended her and got shot. Then it played out again, but in slow motion. Josh wanted to stop time just like he did when Logan brought him here before, but he couldn't. He saw himself walk in the bank. He witnessed the exchange between him and his Spanish tutor. He recognized the warmth he showed toward the pregnant woman. He felt the adrenalin rush when he saw the masked men walk in the bank. He heard his own voice saying how he wished he had some sort of weapon on him to be able to better defend the people around him. He watched every move of the masked men as they walked around the bank with guns drawn.

The scariest part was when the masked gunman was approaching the pregnant woman as she screamed. Every step that he took had an amplified sound as if a giant was walking through the bank. Josh had a split second to make a decision and he did what he thought he should do. He confronted the gunman. In slow motion, the fight played out. Every punch... every grappling move… every struggling moment up until the gun went off. Then everything went black. Total darkness surrounded Josh and Logan.

"What just happened?" Josh asked.

"That's it," Logan answered.

"What's it?" Josh asked.

"Everything… this is it. I've done my job. The rest is up to you."

"I don't get it Logan. You took me back to where it all ended. Well, I guess where it all started. I don't know. This is all so confusing," said Josh.

"You know more than you think you do, Josh. You are a very intelligent man," said Logan.

"What do you mean? I'm floating in outer space, possibly making my ascent into heaven, and all you can say is that I'm intelligent?" Josh yelled!

"Yes Josh, you are very knowledgeable. When you were in the bank, you displayed many of the things you had learned over the years. You had knowledge on how to treat people, how to improvise, you only planted the seeds you wanted to grow when you imagined the fight before it happened. You played full-out, Josh. I could keep going, but why? You know all of these things. You already have all this knowledge," Logan explained.

Josh looked Logan in the eyes and said, "It's all coming together now. It is starting to make sense. Knowledge is great to have, but knowledge is nothing without application. There are thousands of people who have knowledge in our society. Many of them even have specialized degrees. Education is valuable—institutional knowledge and general life knowledge—but it means nothing if it is not applied. A paramedic knowing how to drive an ambulance does nothing for the patient in the back unless he puts the pedal to the metal. Learning is important, but doing is more important. Too many people go to the grave with their treasures still inside of them because they were not in action when they had the opportunity. If you are going to do it, you may as well do it now!"

As soon as Joshua said the last word in the sentence, Logan vanished. No goodbyes, no teleporting Josh back to his small room. He just vanished into thin air. Josh was there... floating... alone... in total darkness. He felt no fear though. He was at peace. He realized that he had no paper to write the lesson he just recited to Logan. All that he could do was close his eyes and fall into a deep sleep.

THE END

What?? Why do you have that look on your face? What else is there? You do know that this is just a story right? If this was a movie, you could imagine your own ending. That way, it can have whatever ending you like. You may have been one of the people that didn't want Josh to die. You were rooting for him the whole time, weren't you? Great! So now you can craft whatever story you want about what happens next.

What did you just ask? Yes, the book is titled, "*31 Amazing Life Lessons of Joshua Stokes*." Oh, we only covered 27? Well, I'm sure some days that Josh visited had more than one lesson in them. Actually, there may be more than "31 things" that you learned already. Oh, I know! What if... what if this was like one of those movies where after all the credits roll, they show more of the film?! Would you like that? If so... then turn the page.

DAY 28

Josh was in the deepest sleep of his life. There was no sound, no light, no anything. Just sleep. He was aware of it, though. It was almost like he could see himself sleeping with total darkness around him. Suddenly, he felt a very sharp pain in his head. It wasn't like the headache he had experienced before. Actually, it was more annoying than painful.

Have you ever been asleep, but you knew something was going on around you during your slumber? Josh was enjoying his rest, but this pain became increasingly agonizing. He sat up suddenly in a cold sweat seeing nothing but a bright light in his face and a body hovering over him. His vision was blurry for a moment, but as soon as he could make out the face in the room with him he spoke.

"Logan? I thought I would never see you again," Josh said.

"I'm sorry Mr. Stokes, my name is not Logan," the gentleman said as he pushed a button in the room.

"What do you mean? And what happened to your wings? Wait, where are we?" Josh asked.

"Sir, my name is Gabriel. I'm Dr. Elkordy's assistant. My mom named me after the angel, but I've never had wings. You are in the hospital, and I was taking out your stitches. Can you please lie back down so that I may finish?"

The room was soon flooded with doctors and nurses from all over the hospital. Dr. Elkordy ran into the room and hugged Josh as if she hadn't seen him in 20 years. Seconds later, Tiffany and Miranda were hugging their dad. Abraham, dressed in a hospital gown, walked in with his doctor and Sarah. His father was going to be just fine. Donavan, Greg, and Dagny and her husband Paul walked in next. [Don't worry, Paul and Josh get along fine. They are actually great friends.]

The room was filled with friends and family. It was a miracle! Joshua Stokes was now awake and the people that he loved were there. He was overwhelmed by the number of people there to greet him. Security was called to his room to try to clear it out, but when they heard his story, all they did was smile and applaud with everyone else. News cameras and reporters started to make their way through the crowd. This was the moment that hundreds of people, if not thousands, had been waiting for. All the news stations wanted to cover this story. They began to ask questions as Gabriel attempted to remove the last few remaining stitches from Josh's scalp.

"Mr. Stokes, Mr. Stokes!" all the reporters begged for the opportunity to ask a question.

"Mr. Stokes… What do you remember? Did you know that you are a hero?" someone asked.

"I don't know if I would call myself a hero. I just did the right thing at the right time," he answered.

"What can you tell us about the bank robbery?" another reporter asked.

"Um, nobody got hurt. That's all I really cared about," Josh replied.

"So what will you do now that you are awake?" a reporter asked.

"I don't know yet. I want to spend time with the people I love. I've also been putting off writing a book for years. That has always been a dream of mine. This whole chain of events made me realize…" Josh didn't finish his sentence.

Everyone in the room was looking at him waiting for him to say something. He started remembering the lessons that he went back to while in his coma. His mind was racing. The reporters didn't know what to do. Gabriel cracked a smile and began to clear the room.

"That's enough ladies and gentleman. Mr. Stokes needs his rest. Only immediate family will be allowed to stay at this time," Gabriel said as he emptied the room of its guests.

Josh grabbed the notepad that was on the table next to his bed. There also were pictures of his girls, next to the notepad. He had something that he really wanted to get on paper, but he was distracted by several items in the room that seemed familiar to him. The pen by his bed was the exact same pen he had used while writing all of the lessons he learned. Gabriel was leaving the room when Josh called him back to ask a question.

"You brought this pen here, didn't you?" Josh asked.

"I know not of what you speak sir," Logan said with a smile.

Josh looked at the inscription on the pen and it read, "From your friend, Captain Obvious. You have work to do." Josh chuckled and began to write:

Feed your dreams: Remember, the Oak Tree sleeps in the acorn. Some of the largest organizations, ministries, movements, and companies in the world were started because someone decided to feed his or her dream. Some of those people didn't even know that their dream would be so big or affect so many people. Some ministries started in someone's living room with just a few people, but now touch hundreds of thousands. George Washington Carver dreamed of the potential of a peanut. Bill Gates and Steve Jobs put millions of computers in homes around the globe because they fed their dreams. There is a chance that hundreds... thousands... even millions of people will live better lives if you decide to FEED YOUR DREAMS!

Just as Josh finished writing, the phone in his hospital room rang. Miranda was the first one to the phone. Though she was the youngest, she was very protective of her father. She was having an in-depth conversation with whoever was on the other end of the phone. With one hand on the phone, and the other on her hip, she made sure she was getting her point across to the other party.

"My Daddy has been sleeping for a long time, and we don't need anybody that he does not know trying to monopolize his time. How did you get this number, ma'am? If I allow you to talk to him, you cannot take up too much of his time. I need him to take me to the zoo, the park, out for ice cream, and possibly to buy me a pony. Oh, we have to go to Hawaii too. Our time is very precious, and we don't want to waste a minute of it," Miranda rambled.

"Miranda Stokes, who are you speaking to like that?" Josh asked.

"I'm sorry; may I have your name again? OK, Dad, it's Karen Forté. You look like you are deep in thought Dad, so I can take a message and you can call her back later if you like," said Miranda.

"How old are you again?" Josh laughed as he held out his hand for the phone.

"This is Joshua Stokes, how may I be of service?"

"Hello, Mr. Stokes. My name is Karen. You have a very intelligent daughter," she said.

"My apologies. She is one of my bodyguards. What can I do for you?" Josh asked.

"I was hoping you could tell me, Josh. I received several envelopes from you," she said.

"Envelopes? I'm sorry, where do I know you from?" asked Josh.

"I don't know that we have ever met. What I do know is that I have had the same mailman for years. His name is Marvin Humes. One day he was delivering my mail, and he apologized for reading a letter addressed to me from you. He said that it wasn't sealed, and it fell out of his bag, so he read it. The note said something about finding a career or business that you can be passionate about, and he left his entire bag of mail on my doorstep. He quit that day and I haven't seen him since. Anyway, I have here on my desk several interesting notes from you. I just started a new publishing company, and I would be interested in flying you to Maryland so that we can figure out a publishing deal with you. By the way, I did some research on you. That was a very brave thing you did at the bank. I was watching the news just now, and I saw that you awoke from your coma today. Welcome back to the land of the living. So, are you interested in discussing a book deal?" Karen asked.

"Ms. Forté, that has always been a dream of mine! I now realize that the only way a dream can come true is if you wake up and work at it. I'm not sure that my doctor will let me travel just yet. I need to focus on my health and my family right now. My birthday is in a few weeks though. I would love to come around the beginning of October if that is OK with you," Josh said with a smile.

Karen agreed to meet with Josh in October. The next few weeks only felt like days to him. His recovery was much faster than the doctors expected it to be. The follow-up stories in the newspapers often labeled him, "The Miracle Man." The pregnant woman from the bank had a baby boy exactly one week after Joshua woke up. You guessed it… she named the baby Joshua. As time drew nearer to Josh's appointment with Karen, he began to have some doubts about the whole thing. Though he had experienced a tremendous amount of success in life, he had never written a book before. It was uncharted territory for him. October was approaching fast, but he made the decision to go.

THE REMAINING LESSONS
LESSON 29

The night before Josh left for Maryland, he was extremely restless. He tossed and turned in bed all night. Sleep eluded him, and he had an early flight to catch. A lack of rest, coupled with the apprehension of possibly writing a book, made Josh a little grumpy. He arrived at the airport on time, but then his flight was delayed. He sat at the gate waiting to board his flight when a very energetic gentleman sat in the seat next to him.

"My apologies, was this seat taken sir?" the gentleman asked.

"No," Josh said with a slight hint of fatigue in his voice.

"Great, my name is Donald Selfston," he said, as he extended his hand toward Josh.

"Joshua Stokes." Josh extended his hand to shake Donald's.

"Joshua Stokes... hmmm... where have I heard that name before?" Donald asked.

"I'm not sure," Josh said to Donald, trying not to be recognized.

A few seconds later, the airline agent announced over the loud speaker that it was time to board the plane. Josh was slightly relieved. Not only was he tired, he didn't want anybody making a big deal about what he did at the bank. He got to his seat on the airplane, pulled out his headphones, and played some relaxing music. He thought that he would at least try to get some sleep on the flight to make up for the sleep he missed the night before. Josh was trying to go to sleep before the flight took off. As soon as he found the perfect classical tune to lull him to sleep, Donald Selfston sat down beside him.

"Looks like lightning can strike the same place twice," Donald said with a smile.

He removed his headphones, so as not to appear rude. "I guess," said Josh with a smirk that looked like it took every drop of energy in his body to muster up.

"I figured it out! You are the guy who saved all those people in the bank. I'm a martial artist as well, and it is a pleasure to meet someone who embodies the true lessons we learn in the dojo," Donald said with excitement.

"No offense Donald, but I am extremely tired. I have a meeting when I land, and I need some sleep. I'm not trying to be rude. I just am not myself right now. Please excuse me," Josh explained.

Donald left Josh alone for the remainder of the flight. Josh slept as best he could. It was a short flight from Chicago to Baltimore, and it felt like he had to wake up as soon as he fell asleep. He put his headphones back on as he was getting off the plane so that he wouldn't have to talk to anyone. With Ludwig van Beethoven playing in his ears, Josh felt as though he was watching a movie unfold in front of his eyes.

Josh was in line waiting to walk through the revolving doors that led to the baggage claim area. Several flights had landed at the same time, so the line was full of impatient travelers who were ready to get on with their day. He turned around to see how far the line was behind him, and Donald Selfston stood about 3 feet back from Josh. Donald noticed that there were two revolving doors available to walk through, but everyone was in line waiting to go through one door. There were no "Out of Order" signs in front of the other door. As a matter of fact, there was nothing to indicate that the door wasn't working.

Donald had a determined look on his face. He couldn't understand why nobody was using the other door. He wasn't an impatient man at all. He was just a man who knew he had a purpose in life. He was the type of person who was not afraid to take the road less traveled. He made the decision that he was going to get out of line a walk past about 100 people who were in line waiting to go through the one revolving door that everyone else was using. With briefcase in hand, he began to walk faster and faster. He strides were strong and deliberate. He walked like he had something to prove; like he was on a mission. He greeted the people he passed with a smile and a look of confidence. When he got to the unused revolving door, he hit it with a stiff-arm that would have pushed aside a professional football player. He let out a huge sigh of relief as the door spun and he walked through it. Within a matter of seconds, several other people got out of the other line and walked toward the door that Donald had just walked through. Josh caught up to Donald at the baggage carousel and decided to speak to him.

"That was fun to watch," Josh said to Donald as he waited for his bags.

"Thanks, sir. I was praying it opened as I walked toward the door!" Donald said.

"What would you have done had it not opened?" Josh asked.

"I would have walked back and stood at the end of the line, but I would have been happy knowing that at least I tried" Donald answered.

"Yeah, that would have been pretty embarrassing," Josh replied.

"I would much rather live with the embarrassment of going for it than the regret of not even trying. I have learned that I cannot let what other people think get to me. Who cares if it didn't open or not?! At least I went for it! I will go to the grave knowing that I lived life everyday making a difference and being an example to those around me. Life is short, Mr. Stokes. Go for it! I don't have to tell you that. You're the guy who took on a gunman in the bank and saved people's lives. Here come my bags, have a good day, sir."

"You're right Mr. Selfston. Life is short. We have to make every moment count!"

Josh immediately opened his briefcase and pulled out his journal. He was looking for a pen so that he could write down what he was thinking, but he couldn't find one. He went through the inside pockets of his suit jacket and found nothing. A custodian was mopping nearby, and he noticed that Josh was looking for a writing instrument. He walked up to Josh, handed him a pen quickly in passing and said, "I think you dropped this."

Josh didn't even get a good look at the guy. When he looked at the pen, there was an inscription that read, "From your friend, Captain Obvious. Don't lose this one!" Josh looked around to try to find him, but Logan... uhh, Gabriel... no, the custodian was nowhere in sight. Josh opened his journal and wrote:

The pain of embarrassment is not as bad as the regret of not trying. People are often afraid to take risks. Too often, we don't take risks because the people around us aren't taking risks. It's easy to follow the masses, but it's more exciting to follow your gut. Don't worry about what people will think or say about you. The only thing that matters is what you think about yourself. Yes, it takes a lot to step out on faith and step out of your comfort zone. Successful people will often do what seems uncomfortable now so that they can get the desired results they want, and live comfortably later.

Don't take life for granted. Make every moment count. I didn't know that the bank would be robbed the day that I walked into it. The people in the World Trade Center didn't know that they would be victims of terrorist attacks on September 11, 2001. We never know what could happen to us. Don't wait for a tragic event in life to wake you up! Live life to the fullest every day, and make every moment count. Remember how Doc Brock cherished every minute of his day? You have to make sure you are filling your days with things that have meaning! We often worry about things that are of no real significance. My request is that you take every day that you have of your life and do something beautiful with it. MAKE EVERY MOMENT COUNT!

Josh closed his journal, located his bags, and proceeded to pick up his rental car.

LESSON 30

Because of the flight delay, Josh didn't have time to go to his hotel before the meeting with Karen. He thought he would have some time to himself to get his thoughts together prior to meeting her. Even successful people get nervous from time to time. After meeting Donald Selfston, Josh knew what he had to do. As he drove toward his destination, he was listening to "The Power of Positive Thinking" by Norman Vincent Peale. Mr. Krouse would have been very proud of him. The words of the audio series gave Josh a sense of peace. It reinforced the things that he already knew. He pulled up to the facility where Karen's office was and the valet took his car. He was escorted through a beautiful atrium to the elevator that would lead him to meet Karen Forté.

"Ahh, Joshua Stokes. It's a pleasure to finally meet you," Karen said as she greeted Josh.

"Thank you Ms. Forté. You have a beautiful facility," replied Josh.

"Thank you, sir. Please come this way to my office."

Karen led Josh down a long hallway with extremely high ceilings. They walked past several pictures of oversized book covers, successful authors, and inspirational quotes. There were trophy cases full of awards from the publishing world. On the wall, next to the huge cherry wood doors of her office hung a blown-up magazine cover with Karen's picture on it. The caption on the magazine read *From Single Mom to Publishing Mogul*.

"Wow, that's impressive!" Josh said as they passed the magazine cover and walked into her office.

"I've been blessed," she said. One of my mentors by the name of Donald Selfston taught me a long time ago that all I needed to do was to become a talent scout. I simply find people with a good story to tell, and I help them tell it," she explained.

"Wait a minute! Donald Selfston? I was just on a plane with him!" Josh exclaimed.

"Yes, I've known him for years. He mentored me to success in another business. He's an amazing family man, and a great friend. I've told him time and time again he needs to write a book. Anyway, let's talk about your book," Karen said.

"I guess a coincidence is God's way of staying anonymous," said Josh.

"Indeed, sir. I have no idea why you sent those notes to me. I was intrigued when I read them. What you wrote has the ability to change lives. I think you just need the proper platform to get it your message out to the masses."

"I don't know, Ms. Forté. I'm far from an author. Yes, I've had some success in my life. I guess I'm a walking miracle right now too. This whole bank incident has shown me a lot. I can't explain how those envelopes got to you. If I told you what I went through while I was in a coma, you would not believe me. Those notes came from… how do I explain… I guess they came from my heart. I don't know how to put it into a book, though. I don't even know if people would be interested in what I had to say," Josh explained.

As they were talking, Karen's personal assistant walked in. She was in her early 20s, and she had a certain posture and air about her that indicated she would do something great in the world. She reminded Josh of his oldest daughter, Tiffany. She was carrying a clipboard in one hand and vase of roses in the other. She walked to

Karen's desk and began to speak. She didn't even pay attention to the fact that Karen was in the middle of a conversation with Josh.

"Mommy, here are the fresh flowers you wanted, and don't forget that you have a traffic court appearance tomorrow. Oh, and the delivery guy is on his way upstairs with the food you ordered," said her assistant.

"I know I taught you better manners than that! We are in the middle of a meeting," Karen responded.

"Sorry, Mommy."

"The LegalShield attorney is handling my court date. Josh, this is Krystal. She is one of my three daughters. This is a family business, and she helps me keep things in order. Krystal, this is Joshua Stokes. He's going to publish a book through us," Karen explained.

"It's a pleasure to meet you, Mr. Stokes. WOW! You look just like my Uncle Mel!" said Krystal.

"No, he does not," Karen replied.

"Stop playing, you know he does mom!" exclaimed Krystal.

Josh said, "It's a pleasure to meet you too, young lady. I'm not sure I will be doing the whole book thing though. I was just explaining to your mom that I am not an author. People may not want to hear what I have to say."

Just as Josh was making his case for why he shouldn't be writing a book, the delivery guy walked in with several bags of food. His load was piled so high, all you could see was the baseball cap that he wore over the top of the bags and boxes he carried. His walked clumsily toward the giant conference table in Karen's office and sat the food down. He began to pull cartons out of the bags and put food onto plates at the table. He acted as if this was his normal routine.

"You certainly do have different delivery guys than we do back in Chicago," said Josh.

"Oh, this is what he does every time he brings us food. I don't mind paying for good service. I was made aware that you are a vegetarian, so I ordered plenty of options for you to select from. I knew that your plane was late, so I figured we didn't need to leave for lunch" Karen explained.

"I'm pretty easy to please," Josh said. "Almost any veggie dish works. Anyway, I don't know if I can do this book thing. Who would want to listen to or read my stuff?" Josh asked.

"Let's ask him," Karen said, as she pointed to the delivery guy.

The gentleman serving the food had his back turned to Karen, Krystal, and Josh. He continued to dish out portions of the delicious-smelling meal. It was a feast fit for a royal family. Josh wondered who was going to eat it all. The gentleman turned around, looked at Josh, and said, "I'm all ears," with a smile on his face. He had on a jacket with the logo of the company he worked for, but under his jacket was an X-Men T-shirt with Wolverine on it.

"Logan?!" said Josh with a smile.

"Yes, that is Logan on my shirt," the gentleman replied. "I'm a huge comic book fan."

"No, you're Logan!" Josh exclaimed.

"No sir, my name is Jesse. If Ms. Forté says you have something worth sharing, I think you should give it a shot. From the conversation I've heard between you all thus far, it seems like you have some exciting stuff to share," said Logan/Gabriel/custodian/Jesse, the delivery guy.

"You know what? Why not?" Josh laughed. "I'll do a book deal with you Ms. Forté. Let me write something down first, and then we can eat and discuss the details."

Josh pulled out his journal and wrote:

You have to share your gifts with others. There are things that only you can do that will have a major impact on the things that you touch. You were created to share the gifts that you have with the people around you. I know, you may have some doubts or worries. That's OK too. Fear is a natural human emotion. Think about it like this though: What if everybody kept their gifts to themselves? Think about your favorite invention, and what life would be like without it. Life without cars, computers, phones, light bulbs, your favorite book, or whatever else you can think of. Some of you may be saying, "Well my gift isn't as significant as the light bulb." I'm here to tell you that you are wrong if you think that way. If you are able to touch just one life, it's worth it. You may be the person that inspires someone else to greatness. SHARE YOUR GIFTS WITH OTHERS!

FINAL LESSON

Hey there! Yes you, my friend. I just wanted to take the time to say thank you for sticking with me. I'm Joshua. Yes, it has been me the whole time taking you on this journey. I thought that the best way to get the lessons across to you were to tell the stories behind them. I was watching you as you were watching me. I apologize if I scared you or offended you in any way. That was not my intent at all. I hope that this was a fun trip for you. I learned long ago that our minds think in pictographs. We think and learn in pictures. I wanted to do my best to paint vivid pictures you could remember. I hope that the lessons you have learned so far will have a lasting impact on your life. My primary goal is to touch the lives of the people I come in contact with. That brings me to the last lesson I have for you. Remember, this is *"31 Amazing Life Lessons: A Journey through the Eyes of Joshua Stokes."*

When you come across a good idea, service, or information, spread the word. For some odd reason, good news does not travel as fast as bad news. Most people are quicker to complain than they are to praise. We will talk about bad service at a restaurant before we talk about the great book we read. When you find something that is helpful to you, or you know will be helpful to others, please spread the word. There are tons of goods and services that could change the world if a few people were fanatical about making sure others knew the stuff existed. So since you have traveled with me this far, I have one thing to ask you before we say goodbye. If you found value in the pages of this book, please share it with other people. Let them borrow yours, or even give them a copy as a gift. The more people who have access to the concepts in this book, the better off the world we live in will become. Again, my primary goal is to have a powerful and positive impact on the lives of the people I touch. That's why I wrote this book.

Again, thank you for sharing my journey with me. It has been a pleasure meeting you, and I look forward to you one day having a story that will help other people in the world. Our lives are not our own. We are designed to make a difference in the world. I love each and every one of you, and there is absolutely nothing you can do about. This isn't the end. This is just the beginning!

# # #

ABOUT THE AUTHOR

A native of Chicago, Mel Roberson is a modern-day anomaly. With an entertaining style and delivery, from the page to the stage, Mel writes and performs from a place of passion, experience, and persistence. As an entrepreneur, he has owned several companies in the business and entertainment industries. As an actor, he has performed in over a dozen films and more than 30 stage plays, even being featured in projects with such notable actors as Tom Sizemore, Karen Malina White, Clifton Powell, and others. As an Amazon.com best-selling author, he has participated in several projects including *The Queens' Legacy* and *Footnotes: A 31-Day Leadership Guide for Women.*

Mr. Roberson's ability to speak and train has landed him on stages across the country in front of crowds as large as 15,000 people, and he has trained tens of thousands of individuals in sales, leadership, and network marketing.

Mel is also very active in the inner city of his hometown, often serving as the keynote speaker at schools and organizations around Chicago. He has a heart for youth and continues to give back to the streets that helped raise him.

Mel's philosophy is that the best is yet to come. He has been quoted as saying, "I just want to be a living example of what is possible with faith, vision, and a little hard work." He loves the quote by Albert Einstein that reads, "The significant problems we face cannot be solved at the same level as when we created them." Because of this, Mel is always looking to enhance his level of thinking, and the thinking of those around him.

For more information on Mel, visit:

www.melroberson.com

FaceBook:

www.FaceBook.com/AmazingLifeLessons

and follow him on Twitter:

www.twitter.com/yesmelroberson

www.theplanforyou.com

CPSIA information can be obtained
at www.ICGtesting.com
Printed in the USA
LVOW11s1138201216
518025LV00001B/1/P